I0796260

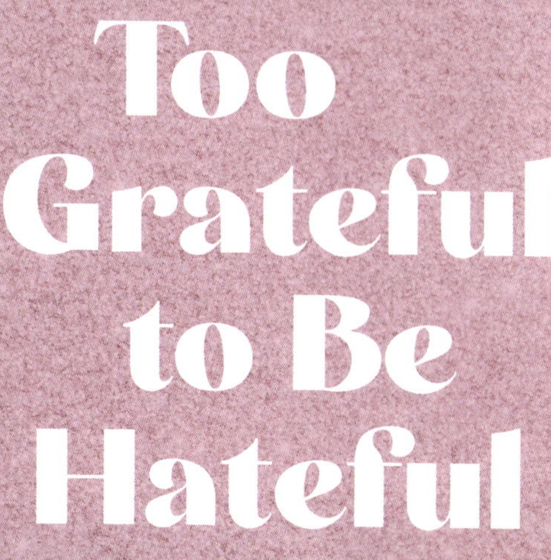

A 365-DAY DEVOTIONAL

BroadStreet
PUBLISHING

BroadStreet Publishing Group, LLC.
Savage, Minnesota, USA
Broadstreetpublishing.com

Too Grateful to Be Hateful

9781424571338
9781424571345 eBook

Devotional entries composed by Natasha Marcellus.

Typesetting and design by Garborg Design Works | garborgdesign.com
Editorial services by Michelle Winger | literallyprecise.com

Printed in China.

25 26 27 28 29 30 31 7 6 5 4 3 2 1

Be thankful in all circumstances,
for this is God's will for you
who belong to Christ Jesus.

1 Thessalonians 5:18 NLT

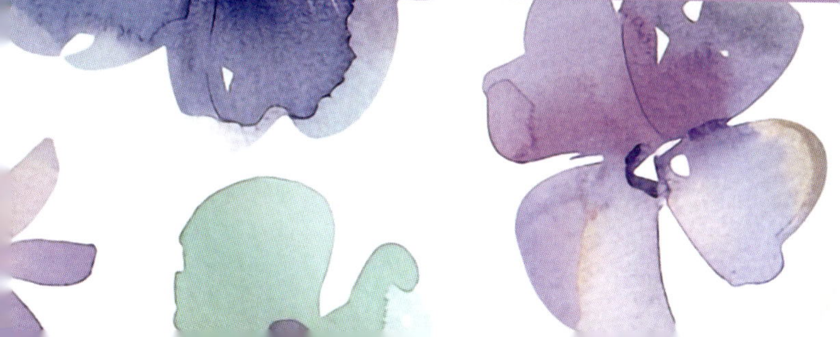

Introduction

In a world where negativity can easily take root, the power of gratitude has the ability to shift your perspective, heal your heart, and transform your relationships. *Too Grateful to Be Hateful* invites you to explore the life-changing practice of gratitude through daily reflections, Scripture, and practical insights.

Each entry will guide you to discover how focusing on the blessings in your life can displace bitterness, anger, and resentment, filling your heart with peace, joy, and compassion. Practicing gratitude not only enhances your relationships, but it also improves your mental and physical health. Whether you're navigating difficult circumstances or simply seeking to strengthen your daily spiritual practices, this devotional will inspire you to cultivate an attitude of thankfulness that will make every moment brighter.

Embrace the beauty of gratitude and find yourself too filled with thanks to hold onto hate.

January

Give thanks for everything to God the Father
in the name of our Lord Jesus Christ.

Ephesians 5:20 NLT

Sing a New Song

Praise the Lord in song,
for He has done glorious things;
Let this be known throughout the earth.

Isaiah 12:5 NASB

God has done glorious things for us. His goodness is unmatched, and his mercy never ends. It's easy to get caught up in what we don't have or the goals we haven't reached yet. We can be fickle and flighty about God's blessings when we should be deliberately thankful.

Taking the time to thank God for everything he's done can shift your attitude from dissatisfaction to contentment. Instead of constantly searching for more, you'll find a sense of steadiness that can only come from knowing you are fully taken care of. Praise God for his mighty work in your life and let your heart be transformed in his presence.

Sing a song of gratitude to the Lord today, recognizing his goodness toward you.

Mercy Alone

It depends not on human will or exertion, but on God, who has mercy.

Romans 9:16 ESV

God's mercy covers a multitude of weaknesses and limitations. His ability to redeem us has nothing to do with what we bring to the table. As we surrender to him, he does the miraculous work of transforming our hearts and setting our feet on solid ground. There aren't any habits or skills that we must master in order for God to save us.

Humility toward God's character and sovereignty is all that's required of you. As you recognize his greatness, he intervenes on your behalf. As you surrender to his ways, he directs your steps. You don't have a greater or lesser ability to follow God than anyone else. Depend on his mercy and he will do the rest.

Instead of trying harder today, trust that God is bigger than your abilities.

Acknowledge Weakness

Immediately the boy's father exclaimed, "I do believe; help me overcome my unbelief!"

MARK 9:24 NIV

Scripture offers a multitude of grace for our humanity. This story in Mark reminds us that God is faithful despite our weaknesses. We can acknowledge where we come up short and trust him to compensate for our limitations. In fact, the presence of a weakness is simply an opportunity for God to be further glorified.

Don't give up on the areas of your life that don't quite measure up. If you struggle to be grateful, don't quit trying. Put your struggles in God's hands and allow him to transform your heart. Acknowledge that you are missing the mark and express your desire for God to move anyway. As you humbly admit your limitations, you make space for God to intervene. He is capable of being faithful in the midst of your greatest flaws.

Ask God for help in believing his truth.

Training Ground

Everyone who competes in the games goes into strict training. They do it to get a crown that will not last, but we do it to get a crown that will last forever.

1 Corinthians 9:25 NIV

If we spend time disciplining our minds and bodies for a goal, how much more should we train our spirits? Living with intention requires being cognizant of how we use our time and where we direct our attention. May we be people of integrity who use our freedom in Christ to transform into his loving image.

Wherever this finds you today, this is your training ground. It's time to take charge and press into the transformative process of focused growth. Look to the Lord and ask him for direction. Trust the guidance of the Holy Spirit and confidently move forward on the path he's given you. Remember that every bit of strength you gain will last forever. Nothing goes to waste in the kingdom of God.

Make a list of three things you can do this week to train your spirit.

Gracious God

In Your great mercy You did not
utterly consume them nor forsake them;
For You are God, gracious and merciful.

NEHEMIAH 9:31 NKJV

Though God is able to create and destroy, his mercy moves him to be patient with us. He is strong to save us from every pit and peril. He does not leave us to waste away in our sin even when we make the wrong choice. He is always close, willing to help us, and full of love that covers our iniquities.

May you be gracious as God is gracious. May you look for ways to extend mercy to others even when they are in situations of their own making. Treat others with the same compassion God bestows upon you. Remember God's great mercy when you are tempted to forsake someone else.

Display God's graciousness by reaching out to a friend to encourage them.

Drenched with Thanksgiving

Return to your rest, my soul,
for the LORD has been good to you.

PSALM 116:7 NIV

When life is chaotic our souls can get caught up in the frenzied pace. In these times, we are not helpless. We can remind ourselves of the peace of God that is available to us here and now. When we are tempted to let worry dictate the confidence of our trust, let's remind our hearts of God's faithful goodness.

You can echo the psalmist's prayer and command your soul to rest. No matter what upsets the calmness of your heart, you can speak peace over yourself. As your heart begins to quiet down you can deliberately recall God's goodness in your life. You can relax and turn toward him with thanksgiving and praise.

Speak peace over the areas of your heart that are struggling to trust God.

Fearless Confidence

The one who lives with integrity lives securely,
but whoever perverts his ways will be found out.

PROVERBS 10:9 CSB

When we live with integrity, there is no need to fear being found out. When we are honest about ourselves and our intentions, there is nothing to hide. Fearless confidence accompanies those who live without deception. Though we are not perfect, there is grace to cover our weaknesses.

Have you ever felt like you needed to hide something about yourself in order to be accepted? The Lord welcomes you with open arms, and he sees your heart clearly. The Father is full of mercy. May you live with honesty and transparency before the Lord and others. You are fully known and fully loved.

Be true to your word and follow through on something you have been putting off.

Never Helpless

No temptation has overtaken you except something common to mankind; and God is faithful, so He will not allow you to be tempted beyond what you are able, but with the temptation will provide the way of escape also, so that you will be able to endure it.

1 Corinthians 10:13 NASB

If we are following Jesus, there is no area in our lives where we are helpless. There is nothing about us that is outside of God's ability to redeem and restore us. Believing that certain sins are inevitable shows that we don't have a full understanding of God's character or mercy. He knows what our weaknesses are, and he gives us what we need to overcome them.

Don't give in to the worldly belief that people cannot change. You are not stuck in destructive patterns or incorrect ways of thinking. God is fully capable of changing your heart and equipping you to follow his ways. If you trust his gentle and kind guidance, he will strengthen you to stand strong no matter what your weaknesses are.

Look to Jesus for help to overcome temptation.

Whatever You Do

Whether you eat or drink, or whatever you do, do all to the glory of God.

1 Corinthians 10:31 NKJV

There is a tendency within Christian culture to elevate certain expressions of worship. We idolize those who speak to large crowds, perform miracles, write books, or live on the mission field. The glorification of certain practices of ministry over others isn't validated in Scripture. Instead, the Word teaches us that everything offered with humility unto God is meaningful.

The life you have right now is incredibly valuable. The way you speak, treat others, and manage your time can be done in the name of God and unto his glory. There is nothing unimportant or insignificant about your life. Every moment of your day is worthy of offering to the Lord.

Worship God with your choices today.

Ask Confidently

"Everyone who asks will receive. The one who searches will find. And everyone who knocks will have the door opened."

Luke 11:10 NCV

God has everything we need, and he is always willing to share the abundance of his kingdom. We can look to him with incredible gratitude because of his joyful provision. We can bring our requests to him with confidence, knowing that he is accessible and generous. He does not turn away anyone who calls on his name.

There is nothing standing between you and God. If you want to be closer to him, there is nothing stopping you. He promises that if you look for him, you will find him. If you knock on the door, he will answer it. His answers to your prayers may not always look how you expect, but he will faithfully do what is best for you. Praise him today for he is reliable and generous.

Bring your requests to God with confidence today.

Healed Hearts

"I will give them one heart, and put a new spirit within them. And I will remove the heart of stone from their flesh and give them a heart of flesh."

EZEKIEL 11:19 NASB

God alone can soften, mend, and redeem our hard and broken hearts. He does this miraculous work because he loves us, and he knows what is best for us. When we give him our rocky and unfruitful ground, he transforms it into rich soil that produces new life. He transforms us in his presence for his glory and our good.

Everything changes when you consistently allow God to cultivate his love into your life. He will faithfully lead you down a path that produces godly character and endurance. He will give you the tools you need to honor him, and he will give you compassion for the people around you. When God's love shapes who you are, there isn't room for hatred, jealousy, frustration, and anxiety.

How have you experienced your heart being softened by God?

Reliable Promise

"I tell you, whatever you ask in prayer, believe that you have received it, and it will be yours."

MARK 11:24 ESV

A promise is only as good as the one who delivers it. When we know someone doesn't keep their word, we don't put stake in what they say. The words they speak don't matter nearly as much as the reliability of their character. In contrast, we can trust what God says because he has proven himself faithful. His promises to fulfill our needs are validated by the way he has intervened on behalf of his children for thousands of years.

When God says you can ask him anything, trust him. When he says he will take care of you, believe what he says. He will not let you down. His love for you is unending, and he is kind and attentive toward you. Step out in faith and ask God for what you need. Don't be afraid to be honest and vulnerable with the one who made you.

Ask, pray, and believe that the Lord will answer you.

Blessed Obedience

"Blessed rather are those who hear the word of God and obey it."

LUKE 11:28 NIV

God doesn't give directions without reason. We can trust that his standards are founded in love and wisdom that is higher than our own. When he gives us instructions, there are always rewards for obedience. We are his children, and he loves to bless us. He promises that we will be blessed when we apply his Word to our lives.

God's blessing in your life might not look exactly how you imagine. Don't discount the internal blessings that come from following him. Peace, contentment, and a sense of belonging cannot compare to any earthly treasure. Ask God how you can apply his Word to your life and thank him for the way he empowers you to do it.

Respond to God's Word with your actions today.

Greater Dependence

"Take my yoke upon you. Let me teach you, because I am humble and gentle at heart, and you will find rest for your souls."

Matthew 11:29 NLT

Jesus is incredibly kind and welcoming. Following him is not a burden. Walking in his ways is not a prison sentence, and it is not beyond our ability. When we feel weighed down by our faith it's time to ask ourselves if we are truly following Jesus. It's possible that we are striving to meet standards that God hasn't asked us to.

God doesn't want you to grit your teeth or muster up your own strength. He wants you to lay your burdens at the foot of the cross. When stress, anxiety, and overwhelm begin to grow, let them be a catalyst to greater dependence on God. Lean on him and let him relieve you of your heaviness. Take a deep breath and be transformed by the peace of his presence.

Spend time in the presence of God listening for his voice and waiting on his peace.

True Satisfaction

Behold, God is my salvation,
I will trust and not be afraid;
For the Lord God is my strength and my song,
And He has become my salvation.

Isaiah 12:2 NASB

As believers we have an unbreakable connection with God. We have access to his peace at all times. We don't need to search the world for answers or frantically try to appease our fears with temporary solutions. We don't need to spend our time searching for purpose or wondering what the future might hold. In every situation we can trust him and rely on his strength.

The world will constantly tell you what you need in order to be satisfied. They'll remind you of what you're lacking and try to feed you the lie that nothing about you or your life is enough. The ways of the world are quickly revealed as meaningless when God is your strength and your song. He alone gives meaning to your life and provides everything you truly need.

How have you searched for satisfaction apart from God?

Bigger Story

The plans of the LORD stand firm forever,
the purposes of his heart through all generations.

PSALM 33:11 NIV

The purposes of God's heart never change. They are consistent, and he is constantly working on them in our lives and in the world. He is full of mercy and loving kindness that meets us where we are. He moves rightly, and he will not neglect his justice. He has been faithful to his promises from generation to generation.

You are part of a story so much bigger than yourself. God's mercy is woven into history, and it doesn't stop with your life. Your life has purpose and meaning. When you recognize that you are an important part of a beautiful masterpiece, your heart will overflow with gratitude. The more you focus on God's story as opposed to what other people are doing, the more peace and contentment you will find.

How does focusing on God's story cultivate peace in your life?

Abundant Joy

With joy you will drink deeply from the fountain of salvation!

Isaiah 12:3 NLT

There is joy in the salvation of the Lord. There is hope in his promises, and there is peace in his presence. There is abundantly more than we could ever need. His love does not run out, and his power is without limitation. There is always more than enough. Let us leave behind our scarcity mindsets and drink deeply from the bottomless well of Christ's mercy.

When was the last time you felt joy at the thought of knowing God? When did you last celebrate being found in him? Remember the gratitude, peace, and pure delight you felt in the beginning of your relationship with him. Remember the freedom that you have been given and the overcoming strength you have access to. May the flame of your abundant joy burn brightly, and may the living waters of God's mercy refresh, restore, and rejuvenate your soul.

Thank God for the gift of his salvation.

Godly Family

Praise the LORD!
I will thank the LORD with all my heart
as I meet with his godly people.

PSALM 111:1 NLT

Being part of the family of God is an incredible gift. We are connected through Christ's sacrifice, and we have the ability to comfort, teach, and help each other. We can spur each other on toward godliness, and we can encourage each other when we are down. Our burdens become lighter when we share them, and we are stronger together than on our own.

Supportive family, faithful friendships, and godly community are reflections of God's goodness in your life. They are an image of his kindness, and they provide a glimpse of the unity you were created for. Praise the Lord for the gift of healthy relationships.

Reach out and thank a faithful friend.

Different Ways

God works in different ways, but it is the same God who does the work in all of us.

1 Corinthians 12:6 NLT

The Lord is the same God he has always been. He is so much greater than our humanity and our understanding. He cannot be relegated to the categories we use for each other. He extends beyond them all. What is created cannot contain the Creator. He is more than the sum of all things.

The diversity of creation reveals the creativity of God. Learning to celebrate the unique expressions of divine love in each other's lives is a blessing! God works in a wonderful variety of ways and limiting him just prevents you from seeing the full picture of his love. Seek to expand your understanding and continually discover how vast he is.

Remember that our differences aren't what's most important about us.

Loving Correction

Such love has no fear, because perfect love expels all fear. If we are afraid, it is for fear of punishment, and this shows that we have not fully experienced his perfect love.

1 John 4:18 NLT

The love of God is more powerful than any other force in this world. It is greater than fear, more potent than hate, and it is constantly pushing back the boundaries of our limited understanding. When we are afraid, it is not because of the Lord.

When you are awaiting punishment for your slip-ups and failures, you cannot move in the true freedom of God's love. He sets you free to transform and grow in his wisdom without fear of failure. He will correct you, but even his correction builds up rather than tearing down. He sees you perfectly, and he knows what is best.

Do you fear correction from God?

Common Good

To each is given the manifestation of the Spirit for the common good.

1 Corinthians 12:7 ESV

God does not overlook his children. He does not withhold his Spirit from some and give freely to others. We all receive from the same abundance. His power is equally accessible, and he gives out mercy and grace without limitation. It simply looks different in each of our lives.

God's love for you is the overarching reason for everything he does. When you are tempted to compare your life to others, remember that God is sovereign and perfectly wise. You can trust his plans even when things look different than how you might prefer.

How have you seen the manifestation of the Spirit in your own life?

Nothing Hidden

"Your Father, whom you cannot see, will see you. Your Father sees what is done in secret, and he will reward you."

MATTHEW 6:18 NCV

Our unseen actions matter. Our hearts are revealed by the things we do when we think no one is looking. God sees every sacrifice and act of love. What is done in secret is plain to him, and he will not fail to reward us for the integrity we choose.

Don't give in to the idea that the small things in life don't matter. How you choose to live when no one is watching is as important as how you present yourself to others. When your hidden life matches what is seen, contentment and confidence are born. Authenticity allows you to remain open and humble before the Lord and others.

How can you cultivate authenticity in your everyday life?

Unique and Free

The body does not consist of one member but of many.

1 Corinthians 12:14 ESV

We are each unique reflections of God's image. He does not expect us all to look the same. His vast nature is displayed in the diversity of the universe. He is endlessly creative, and that applies as much to us as it does to the details of the earth. We were each thoughtfully and wonderfully made.

Have you been striving to become like others, denying parts of yourself in the process? God wants you to experience the freedom that comes from embracing who he made you to be. You are not meant to conform to the patterns of this world, and that includes blending into systems, communities, and friend groups where you have to hide who you are. Ask God for his perspective on your life.

Embrace God's definition of who you are and allow others to freely be themselves.

Stay the Course

Do not turn aside; for then you would go after empty things which cannot profit or deliver, for they are nothing.

1 Samuel 12:21 NKJV

Goals and visions keep us moving. When we are working toward something, we are constantly motivated by the desire to complete our goal. Even when challenges arise, we choose to persevere when the goal is more important than the struggles we might face. Scripture says that people perish without vision.

If you feel lost at sea in this season of your life, having no clear vision for the future, rest in God's presence and ask him for his perspective. The goal you move toward doesn't need to be lofty or wild. Getting through the day might be enough. Learning how to lean on the Lord in a deeper way might be enough. No matter what God puts before you, stay the course and trust his leadership.

Keep turning your thoughts to Jesus throughout your day.

People of God

The LORD will not abandon His people on account of His great name, because the LORD has been pleased to make you a people for Himself.

1 SAMUEL 12:22 NASB

The Lord promises to never abandon his people. He vows to always be with us. His kingdom is inclusive, and he welcomes all with the same powerful love. It is his delight to make us a people for himself. He draws us in with kindness, and he calls us his own.

Have you submitted your life to the love of Jesus? Then you are his! He is close when you are broken-hearted, and he is near when you rejoice in celebration. What a wonderful kingdom you have been ushered into. There is more to discover in his great love!

Praise God for calling you his own.

All Your Heart

"Only fear the Lord and serve him faithfully with all your heart. For consider what great things he has done for you."

1 Samuel 12:24 ESV

Where your heart is, there will be your treasure. Jesus' words resound with truth. They are as applicable today as they were when he first spoke them. When we give God access to our whole hearts, leaning into the fellowship we have with his Spirit through Christ, we are transformed by his living love.

When we submit our lives to the Lord, we give him the right to lead us. When we get to know the beautiful and merciful nature of God, we cannot help but to love him. Why would we strike out on our own when companionship with the Creator of all things is ours? What great things he does for us! What abundant mercy he shows us.

Consider how good God has been to you and give him access to your whole heart.

Rediscover Wonder

Since we are receiving a kingdom that cannot be shaken, let us be thankful, and so worship God acceptably with reverence and awe.

HEBREWS 12:28 NIV

Though power dynamics in this world rise and fall, the kingdom of God is unshakable. When we partner with God in prayer and in our lifestyles, we invite heaven to invade earth through the coming of his kingdom.

Jesus performed miracles of mercy that changed people's lives forever. He promised that we would do even greater things. Are we living in the power of his presence? Let's not grow weary in uniting with the Lord in his purposes. He knows best, and we can trust his wisdom. Jesus will one day return with the fullness of his glorious victory. Let's not lose sight of his coming!

Meditate on the coming kingdom of God and thank him for his perfect wisdom.

Trust Him

"Don't be concerned about what to eat and what to drink. Don't worry about such things."

LUKE 12:29 NLT

God is our good, good Father. He does not offer his children stones when we ask for bread. He does not trick us by offering one thing and switching it out at the last moment. He is honest, kind, and transparent. He has what we need, and he will take care of us.

When you struggle to trust, ask for his help. Don't hesitate to look for encouragement in trusted friends and fellow lovers of God. What God has done for others, he will also do for you. His faithful nature will never fail.

Stop striving and give God your worries.

Cared For

"The Gentile world eagerly seeks all these things, and your Father knows that you need them."

Luke 12:30 CSB

We cannot exaggerate the love of God. We can't overstate his goodness. He is infinitely better than we could ever describe. He is good, and he is for us. We can turn toward him in every circumstance. As he meets us, we will grow in deeper confidence and trust.

Lay aside your worries today. Lay down thoughts of how you will get from where you are to where you need to be. God is a faithful leader, and he will not let you down. He offers you help, strength, and provision through every season of your life. When you cannot see a path forward, fix your attention on the Lord.

Rest in the tender attentiveness of your Father.

Godly Longings

Earnestly desire the greater gifts.
And yet, I am going show you a far better way.

1 Corinthians 12:31 NASB

God gives freely to all who ask. It is good to earnestly desire the gifts he offers us. There is nothing holding us back from growing in the areas of healing, teaching, and prophecy. God promises that if we cultivate these things, he will help us.

God has given you gifts that are meant to help the people around you. As you lay your life down for others, offering them your time, talents, and resources, you show them what God's love looks like. If you want to grow in your ability to help people, God will not abandon you. He loves it when you seek to love more like he does.

Let the desire for more of God's power in your life lead you to ask him for greater gifts.

Humble Love

Love is patient and kind. Love is not jealous or boastful or proud.

1 Corinthians 13:4 NLT

The love of God is humble. It does not seek to be right. It does not put down others in order to be lifted up. It is not in a rush, and it is always kind. It uplifts the lowly and heals the broken. It is powerful, restorative, and full of hope.

What kind of love do you live by? Is compassion evident in your life? Are you patient with others and humble in your exchanges with them? Today, look to Jesus to see what laid-down love resembles. His love is full of peace, confidence, and trust. May Christ's endless love be your foundation for every relationship and interaction.

Choose to be patient with others today, knowing that God is patient with you.

February

Enter his gates with thankgiving;
go into his courts with praise.
Give thanks to him and praise his name.

PSALM 100:4 NLT

Your Response

You shall follow the LORD your God and fear Him; and you shall keep His commandments, listen to His voice, serve Him, and cling to Him.

DEUTERONOMY 13:4 NASB

Following the Lord is as simple as responding to what he has already done. His character does not change, and he is always faithful. We don't have to guess what he's like or wonder how he might respond to us. The only variable in our relationship with him is us. We get to choose if we will listen to his voice, serve him, and cling to him.

God's pursuit of you never changes. He is consistent in the way he loves you and how he responds to you. If you want to have a closer relationship with him, you must choose to be intentional in your pursuit of him. Get to know his character, read the Word, and ask questions to other believers. Be inspired by God's faithfulness in your life and in the lives of those around you. As you pursue him throughout your day, you'll find that he is more involved in the details of your life than you think.

How can you simplify your pursuit of God?

No Record

[Love] keeps no record of wrongs.

1 Corinthians 13:5 niv

If Scripture teaches that love keeps no record of wrongs and that God is the embodiment of love, we can trust that God himself does not keep a record of wrongs. When we give him our sins, he makes us clean. He forgives us, and he removes our transgressions from us. He doesn't even remember them.

When you make mistakes, God is not frustrated that you've done it again. He's not wondering why you can't seem to get it together. Every single time you repent and ask forgiveness he approaches you with abundant mercy. This is why it matters so much that you run to him with your sins. You may be tired of making the same mistake, but God will never grow weary of you approaching him for help.

How has fear or shame kept you from approaching God with your struggles?

No Room

Be content with what you have,
because God has said,
"Never will I leave you;
never will I forsake you"

HEBREWS 13:5 NIV

When we practice contentment, we will become more focused on God's provision than what we lack. As we learn to thank him for all the ways he's provided for us, we become less preoccupied with the things our neighbors have. There is no room for comparison, jealousy, or dissatisfaction when your heart is turned toward God in gratitude.

Don't compare your life to anyone else's. Don't spend time wondering why someone else has what you want or why certain parts of your life aren't how you imagined they would be. Instead, ask God to show you the goodness in your own life. Loving the life you have is fully within your control. As you keep your eyes on the Lord and deliberately cultivate the habit of gratitude, you'll notice that your greatest gift is God's presence in your life.

Write a list of what you are thankful for in this moment.

Carried Through

Love never gives up, never loses faith, is always hopeful, and endures through every circumstance.

1 Corinthians 13:7 NLT

God never gives up. He never loses faith. He is always hopeful, and he endures through every circumstance. When we are weary and feel as if we cannot go on, God offers us the strength of his love. When everything goes wrong and we can't find relief from our pain, we can lean on him and trust him to take care of us. In every circumstance, God's love remains.

Your relationship with God gives you an internal strength that cannot be taken away from you. He will keep you steady when it doesn't make sense to be strong. He will carry you through trials that seem impossible and far beyond your depth. His love for you will hold you up when all you want to do is crumble under the weight of your trials. You can endure through every circumstance because God is love, and he never fails.

How can you depend on God's love today?

Reliable Love

Love never fails.

1 CORINTHIANS 13:8 NCV

God's love is the strongest force in the universe. His love is not flimsy; it is strong. His love is reliable, capable, and all-encompassing. Everything God does is built upon a foundation of love. He cannot be separated from his love.

God's love is worth all your time, resources, and abilities. It is the most valuable pursuit you will ever embark upon. There is nothing worth more than the unfailing love of God. It doesn't matter what your title is, what you accomplish, or how other people perceive you. God's love is wroth everything you have.

How can you devote yourself further to the pursuit of God's unfailing love?

Firm Foundation

Jesus Christ is the same yesterday and today and forever.

Hebrews 13:8 NASB

It can be challenging to find stability in a world that is always shifting and changing. Relationships end, cultural standards ebb and flow, and societies crumble. It's fitting to point out that change is the only reliable aspect of the human condition. Instead of growing weary or feeling like we can't keep up, we have the incredible gift of God's steady character.

Reflect on Christ's unchanging nature with gratitude. Relax in his presence and remember that he is steady when nothing else is. He is reliable, strong, and trustworthy. When the world is shaking, he is unmoving. When you feel swept away by the current of world events, he is your solid rock and firm foundation.

How can the reliability of Jesus change your perspective of the world?

Keep Growing

When I was a child, I used to speak like a child, think like a child, reason like a child; when I became a man, I did away with childish things.

1 Corinthians 13:11 NIV

As we mature, we adapt our thinking to include a broader understanding of the world and its ways. A child may look at the moon and see a face, thinking a man lives there. As they grow and learn, they put away the fantastical thought of a personified moon. The same thing is true about our relationship with God.

Your faith will grow and mature the longer you follow the Lord. Your perspective will shift, and you'll gain wisdom. It's important to be able to set aside something you previously believed when you are confronted with a broader understanding. Change requires humility because you must be able to admit that you aren't the final authority on the ways of God. Remain humble and open to the process of maturing.

How have you resisted growth in the past?

Above All Else

Three things will last forever—faith, hope, and love—
and the greatest of these is love.

1 Corinthians 13:13 NLT

Do we consider others more important than ourselves? Do we elevate our own comfort over kindness? Do we let our limited scope of understanding keep us from acting in compassion? Whatever we do, whether in word or in deed, may we do it with trust in God's faithfulness and hope in his promises. May his love be our unshakable foundation and ultimate motivation.

If you are tired of being reminded of the importance of love, perhaps what you need today is a fresh revelation of its power. There truly is nothing more indicative of God and his kingdom than the strength of his love. When it all boils down, what is left? Faith, hope, and love. How do these show up in your life?

Make love the goal of your interactions today.

Beautiful Fruit

By Him let us continually offer the sacrifice of praise to God, that is, the fruit of our lips, giving thanks to His name.

Hebrews 13:15 NKJV

When we feel like we don't have anything meaningful to offer God, we can shift our perspective by reminding ourselves of the truth. Hebrews says that the fruit of our praise is a sufficient sacrifice. God doesn't want our skills or talents. He doesn't want our accomplishments or successes. Instead, he asks us for the praise of our lips and a heart that is thankful.

Your words are an act of worship. When you approach God with thanksgiving not only does it transform your heart, but it shows that you have an accurate understanding of who he is and what he's done for you. Tell God what you are thankful for and speak kindly and truthfully. Look for opportunities today to practice offering God the fruit of your words.

Think about what you say before you speak.

Confidence in Christ

"Don't worry or surrender to your fear. For you've believed in God, now trust and believe in me also."

JOHN 14:1 TPT

Jesus is the way, the truth, and the life. He is the peace in every storm. He is the loyal love that covers us at all times. He is our Savior who has broken the chains of fear and shame. He is our liberator and our Redeemer. He is the one who was, who is, and who is to come. He is constant in mercy, consistent in grace, and full of unmatched power.

What fears are keeping you from moving forward in peace? Give them to Jesus because he is more than able to carry the weight of your burdens. You are not alone in your struggles, and you are not isolated in your troubles. Jesus is with you. His Spirit is your source of strength, hope, and love. There is more than enough peace in his presence both now and forever.

How can you surrender to Jesus rather than fear today?

Abundant Life

"I am the way, the truth, and the life. No one can come to the Father except through me."

JOHN 14:6 NLT

Jesus paved the way to the Father. When we look at the Son, he is the living expression of the Father's love. There is no other way for us to find belonging and satisfaction than through Christ. He alone fulfills the longing of our hearts. He alone has made a way for us to be with our Maker.

No matter what you think you need, you were made for nearness to God above all else. Searching for love, happiness, satisfaction, or success in any place other than God will eventually leave you disappointed. God is the source of everything you really need. Let your heart overflow with thanksgiving because Jesus has opened the door to the eternal security and blessing of the kingdom of God.

Thank Jesus for providing for your greatest needs.

Always Hope

There is hope for a tree, if it is cut down,
that it will sprout again,
and that its tender shoots will not cease.

JOB 14:7 NKJV

A healthy tree can withstand seemingly devastating circumstances. It continues to sprout and grow even when it is cut down. This is how God describes us when we are rooted and grounded in his love. He assures us that even when we think there isn't hope, he will keep us in a position where we thrive and produce fruit. We are safe under his watch.

No matter the destruction you have experienced in your life, the Lord your God will redeem and restore you. He does not ignore your cries for help. He does not turn away from you in your grief. If there is hope for a tree to sprout again, how much more hope is there for you to experience renewal? Put your trust in him, for he is able to do far more than you can even imagine.

Speak hope over any despair you feel and trust God to restore you.

Peace and Joy

The kingdom of God is not eating and drinking, but righteousness and peace and joy in the Holy Spirit.

ROMANS 14:17 NASB

Thank God that our relationship with him is not about our habits and actions. He doesn't look at our behavior and declare us worthy of his love or not. We aren't welcomed into his family based on our ability to follow the house rules. Instead, we are welcomed in because he desires unbroken fellowship with us. He adopts us into his family and gives us righteousness, peace, and joy in the Holy Spirit.

When you embrace how God sees you, you can extend the same grace to others. When you experience God's beautiful mercy, you can love others with less judgment and more compassion. God doesn't hold you to a standard you cannot keep, and you will find freedom when you refuse to do the same toward others. Let your heart overflow with thanksgiving toward God for drawing you into his family and loving you with unending compassion.

Look for the fruit of the Spirit outside of rules and regulations today.

Greatest Gift

"The Helper, the Holy Spirit, whom the Father will send in My name, He will teach you all things, and bring to your remembrance all things that I said to you."

John 14:26 NKJV

As believers we are never alone. We have the help of the Holy Spirit at all times and in all circumstances. He is a gift to us from Jesus. We can trust his guidance because Jesus himself said that he would teach us everything and remind us of what's true. There is no reason for us to flounder or struggle through life when we have an advocate, teacher, and encourager within us.

The presence of the Holy Spirit is an indication of God's incredible provision in your life. He knows every single trial you will face, and he has provided you with everything you need. He knows what each of your days will entail, and he has given you a companion who will never leave you. Recognize the gift of the Spirit and your struggles will seem less catastrophic as you realize you are more than equipped to handle them.

Ask for a fresh revelation of the gift of the Spirit.

Abundant Peace

"Peace I leave with you; my peace I give you. I do not give to you as the world gives. Do not let your hearts be troubled and do not be afraid."

JOHN 14:27 NIV

We were not created to embrace chaos or suffer through stress and anxiety. We might stubbornly insist on carrying our own burdens, but God has offered us a different way. He gives us peace in abundance anytime we ask for it. He does not expect us to fearfully walk through our days. When we depend on him, he gives us the supernatural ability to endure trials with a steady heart.

The world's peace is temporary and unsustainable. Worldly peace depends on circumstances and your own actions while godly peace is internal and cannot be shaken. The world says you can find peace or even manufacture it. God says that peace is a gift that he gives without discrimination. There's no need to frantically search for something that is abundantly available by the hand of God. Run to him with thanksgiving and let his peace saturate every part of your life.

How have you tried to manufacture your own peace?

Clarity

God is not a God of confusion but of peace.

1 Corinthians 14:33 ESV

This passage in 1 Corinthians addresses the way we behave in church. There was concern that a lack of order would frustrate and confuse those who were listening. The encouragement we find in Scripture is that God loves order and clarity. He offers us peace in the midst of confusion. He is never frantic, overwhelmed, or over stimulated. Everything he does is calm, calculated, and full of peace.

If you've ever been in a chaotic church setting, you know how disorienting it can be. Remember that God has not created you to thrive in that type of environment. It's okay to question a lack of order and the presence of confusion. Ask God to bring clarity and he will.

When you are confused, ask God for the clarity of his ways.

His Battle

The Lord is my strength and my defense;
he has become my salvation.
He is my God, and I will praise him,
my father's God, and I will exalt him.

Exodus 15:2 NIV

God alone is our strength and our defense. He doesn't ask us to take up arms and fight for ourselves. He asks us to humbly put our lives in his hands and trust that he is capable of defending us. He asks us to lay down our weapons and trust his power and might. This can be difficult to do if we are accustomed to pulling up our bootstraps and gritting our teeth through the trials of life.

If you're the type of person who has always had to look after yourself, you might find it difficult to surrender to the Lord. He longs for you to stop striving and trust him. He longs for you to relax and lean on his leadership over your own. He delights in giving you strength and grace whenever you need it. Instead of being filled with rage against a multitude of enemies, let the Lord soften your heart and lead you toward surrender.

How have you been fighting your own battles lately?

Simply Remain

"Remain in me, as I also remain in you. No branch can bear fruit by itself; it must remain in the vine. Neither can you bear fruit unless you remain in me"

JOHN 15:4 NIV

God offers us continuous connection with him. He is the vine, and we are the branches. No matter what is going on in our lives, we can stay secure and at rest in his presence. It's easy to lose sight of the power of being connected to Christ. We are easily distracted by our toils and the challenges of the world. If we remain in him, we will find that our hearts will overflow with thankfulness for his love, grace, and provision.

Your unbroken connection with God is possible because of Jesus. You have access to everything you need at all times. When you are tempted to focus on what you don't have, remember that God has promised to provide for you as you seek him and his purposes. Rely on the connection you have with the Lord when your flesh rises up to complain.

How can focusing on your connection with God cultivate gratitude in your life?

Each One

"If a man has a hundred sheep and one of them gets lost, what will he do? Won't he leave the ninety-nine others in the wilderness and go to search for the one that is lost until he finds it?"

Luke 15:4 NLT

God is incredibly attentive. He is aware of each person's struggles, hurts, and triumphs. He knows what we each need, and he knows the perfect path to lead us closer to him. God does not write off any of his children or decide that they aren't worth his time or sacrifice. He sees each of his children with great affection and value.

Your specific and unique life matters. You are not insignificant or without purpose. It's easy to lose sight of the big picture and begin to feel as though your life isn't having as big of an impact as you'd like. Remember that God sees just as much value in a single life as in the multitude of the whole. He has not overlooked you or forgotten about you.

Remind yourself of the truth of God's attentiveness when you feel forgotten.

God's Gift

Such things were written in the Scriptures long ago to teach us. And the Scriptures give us hope and encouragement as we wait patiently for God's promises to be fulfilled.

ROMANS 15:4 NLT

It's important to remember that Scripture was written for our benefit. When we overlook its power, we cut ourselves off from God's gift of encouragement, hope, and wisdom. When we allow the truth of Scripture to saturate our lives, we experience the blessing, contentment, and satisfaction of following God's best plan for our lives.

Waiting for God's promises to be fulfilled isn't always easy. Trudging through difficult situations or mundane days can take a toll. Lean on the solid foundation of Scripture in the midst of your struggles. Use it to lift you up and bring you comfort when you need it most. Immerse yourself in the Word and walk by its wisdom.

How can you incorporate more scriptural truth in your life?

Sacrificial Love

"There is no greater love than to lay down one's life for one's friends."

JOHN 15:13 TPT

When we embrace sacrificial love like Jesus did, we discover transformative power that is greater than hatred or selfishness. Not only do we reflect Christ to others when we lay down our lives, but we ourselves are transformed. Bitterness, a lack of gratitude, and disdain for others cannot remain when we actively choose to put the needs and wants of others before our own.

Reflect on the power of love and sacrifice within your own life. It's likely that you've felt most loved when someone else laid aside their own preferences or comfort in favor of yours. When a friend makes time to comfort you in your grief, even when their life is full, you feel noticed. When a family member listens intently rather than debating their own point, you feel heard and empowered. There is immense power in setting aside what you want in order to lift up someone else.

How can you give preference to someone other than yourself today?

The Greatest Treasures

May the God of hope fill you with all joy and peace as you believe so that you may overflow with hope by the power of the Holy Spirit.

Romans 15:13 CSB

God does not ask us to give up our lives without giving us something in return. He does not demand obedience and leaves us empty handed. In fact, what we receive from him far outweighs anything we can give. When we trust in him, he gives us abundant joy and peace. When we devote our lives to his ways, he allows us to walk in the power of the Holy Spirit which fills us with hope.

When the opulence and allure of the world seem overwhelming, remember what God offers you. It's normal to be tempted by the promise of personal satisfaction and instant gratification. Take time to meditate on God's incredible generosity and allow your heart to overflow with gratitude. As you consistently turn your eyes toward him, both the trials and temptations of the world will become less of a burden.

Look to the Lord and remember that what he offers is greater than any worldly treasure.

He Chooses

"You did not choose Me but I chose you, and appointed you that you would go and bear fruit, and that your fruit would remain."

John 15:16 NASB

God is a relentless pursuer. His faithful pursuit of his people is the great equalizer. He does not pick one over the other, and he doesn't choose us based on our own merit. When we acknowledge God's work in our lives, it's only natural to be filled with gratitude. He consistently does what we cannot. He draws us close, transforms our hearts, and gives us eternal freedom.

Even on your best day, it's important to remember that God chose you. He wasn't swayed by your skills, and he didn't turn away because of your weaknesses. Your pursuit of him is only possible because he has been pursuing you all along. Instead of finding confidence in your own abilities, humbly acknowledge that he alone has chosen and appointed you to reflect his image.

Thank God for loving you first, choosing you, and being the source of every good gift.

Turn Back

"So he returned home to his father. And while he was still a long way off, his father saw him coming. Filled with love and compassion, he ran to his son, embraced him, and kissed him."

LUKE 15:20 NLT

God is consistent and reliable. We can bet everything on the fact that he will run to us with overflowing joy every time we turn to him. No matter how far away we've wandered, we can count on him being delighted to see us. Even when we've willingly walked away from him, he welcomes us back with open arms. He celebrates our meagre acts of faithfulness as though we've conquered the world.

If you are searching the world for validation, you will come up wanting. If you are looking around for someone to tell you that you are valuable, you will never be satisfied. Why look anywhere else but the loving embrace of your Father? He created you, knows you inside out, and longs for you to experience the fullness of his love. He is eternally compassionate toward you every time you acknowledge him.

Allow God's faithful and joyful love to fill you with gratitude.

Shared Burden

"O death, where is your victory? O death, where is your sting?"

1 Corinthians 15:55 ESV

While we experience the grief of death during this life, we can confidently remember that the pain will not last forever. God has declared that death will not win. Death will not have the final word. Even when we are lost in grief, we can rely on the fact that better days are coming.

Grief may be an unwelcome burden, yet it is not yours to carry alone. God offers you the comfort of his presence and the reassurance of his promises. Lean on the Lord no matter what or who you are grieving. Offer him the full scope of your pain, the messiness of your emotions, and the weariness of your soul. Allow him to comfort you and give you hope even when it seems impossible to look even one day into the future.

Offer your losses to God and allow him to comfort you.

Through Christ

Thanks be to God! He gives us the victory through our Lord Jesus Christ.

1 Corinthians 15:57 NIV

All our personal defeats are covered by the overcoming power of Christ's love. He restores what was taken from us, and he redeems the time that we have lost. He leads us toward reconciliation and peace. He gives us wisdom, and he teaches us how to live.

Though we may struggle to forgive ourselves, God fully forgives us when we turn to him and repent. His victory becomes our victory. There is more life ahead than any destruction we leave behind. He is our help, our strength, and our deliverer. He moves in mighty miracles of mercy, and he will not stop!

Thank Jesus for his overcoming power today.

Each Moment

My dear brothers and sisters, stand strong. Do not let anything move you. Always give yourselves fully to the work of the Lord, because you know that your work in the Lord is never wasted.

1 Corinthians 15:58 NCV

When we devote our lives to God, we can trust that every moment counts. He sees every act of faith, service, and sacrifice. He is proud of us when we honor his Word, and he gently encourages us when we make mistakes. He leads us with wisdom, and he comforts us when we grieve. He is faithful and consistent to work in our lives, and our work in his name is never overlooked.

When you feel insignificant, remember that God sees you. When you feel unnoticed, remember that God is aware of each moment of your life. Not a single thing goes to waste. You can persevere through trials because you know that every act of faith, big or small, matters to God. He is so proud of you when you cling to hope, even when it feels like you are hanging on by a thread.

Take heart and be motivated by the value of every moment.

He Sees

"The LORD does not see as man sees; for man looks at the outward appearance, but the LORD looks at the heart."

1 SAMUEL 16:7 NKJV

If we want to embrace the true beauty of creation, we must look at the heart. The soul and character of a person matter so much more than how we perceive them. Our society often prioritizes outward experiences, but as believers we know that true value comes from within. We honor God when we imitate him and look past the obvious and fleshly attributes of people.

God sees you exactly as you are. He cannot be manipulated by your best attempts to present yourself in a certain way. He knows your greatest flaws, and he still looks at you with incredible love and kindness. Learning to look at others in this way is life changing. When you write someone off because of their weaknesses, you miss out on the opportunity to love them with the transformative love of Jesus. The more you look past outward appearances and into the hearts of others, the less room you will have for hatred, comparison, and judgment.

Thank God for how he sees you.

March

Devote yourselves to prayer with an alert mind and a thankful heart.

Colossians 4:2 NLT

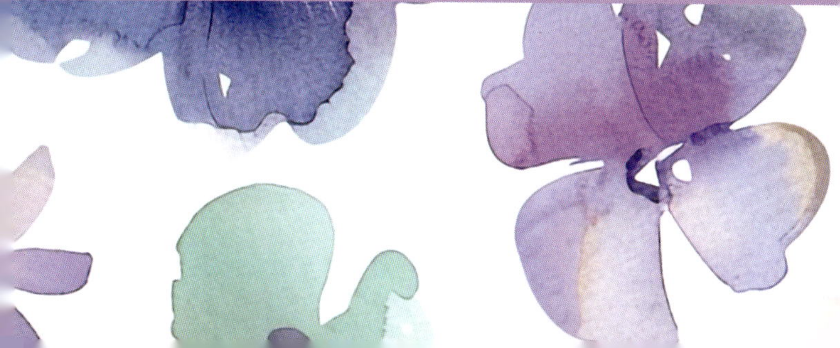

Spirit of Truth

"When the Spirit of truth comes, he will guide you into all truth. He will not speak on his own but will tell you what he has heard."

John 16:13 NLT

We are not waiting for the Spirit of truth to come to us. He already has! The Spirit of God is the one who guides us into the truth of God's kingdom. Just as Jesus spoke on behalf of the Father, the Spirit speaks on behalf of the Father and Son. They are united and one in love.

If you are struggling to know which way to go or what to do in the midst of confusion, ask the Spirit to guide you with his clarifying wisdom. Seek out the advice of trusted advisors. Do what you know to do and be open to letting new information adjust your understanding. Wherever you are, you have access to the fullness of God through his Spirit.

Ask the Spirit to speak to you as you read the Word.

All in Love

Do everything with love.

1 Corinthians 16:14 NLT

The overarching theme of love is threaded through the message of Jesus. He spoke of treating others the way we want to be treated. The way we love others is an overflow of the love we receive from God. Love is not always an easy choice. Turning the other cheek or laying down our defenses won't always feel natural, but it is always worth it.

Christ's love transforms all who experience it. The discomfort we might feel is temporary, but the impact of his love is eternal. We have the privilege and opportunity to offer people the same life transforming love that God has offered us. Instead of withholding that gift, we should give it freely and abundantly. May we choose love in all that we do, humbling ourselves before God and others.

Approach today's mundane tasks with an attitude of love.

Complete Joy

"Until now you have not asked for anything in my name. Ask and you will receive, and your joy will be complete."

John 16:24 NIV

Jesus continuously invites us into a deeper relationship with him. He encourages us to express our faith through prayer and gratitude because he knows that those things will draw us closer to him. He doesn't ask us to approach him out of obligation or subservience. Instead, he promises us full and complete joy when we align ourselves with his heart.

If your heart feels lost in bitterness, hatred, frustration, or confusion, run to Jesus. Ask for healing in his name and allow him to direct your steps. Walk humbly along the path he shows you and trust that he will faithfully replace your heart of stone with one of flesh. He will give you joy, peace, and love in exchange for your surrendered heart. As you trust him to do what only he can, he will not let you down.

Ask God for help today and trust that he will provide it.

Loosen Your Grip

"If you try to hang on to your life, you will lose it. But if you give up your life for my sake, you will save it."

MATTHEW 16:25 NLT

The tighter our grip on our own lives, the more anxiety and pride will grow in our hearts. The more we think that we are in control and that our strength has sustained us, the further we will fall when our beliefs are challenged. Jesus invites us to give up control and surrender to him. He knows that when we let go, we find true freedom and contentment.

What is holding you back from fully giving your heart to Jesus? Are you afraid of what he might ask you to do? Have your experiences taught you that you can only rely on yourself? Any hesitation to trust Jesus simply stems from a misunderstanding of his character. Remember that he is faithful, true, just, and kind. He knows what is best for you, and he longs for you to experience the joy of surrender.

How can you trust God with the details of your daily life?

Wholly Loved

"The Father himself loves you."

John 16:27 NIV

There is nothing about you that falls outside of the loving embrace of your Father. He is the one who fights for your freedom and draws you to himself in kindness. Even his correction is lined with love. Though you may struggle to accept the failures you have experienced, there is nothing that God cannot redeem and restore. He is a master at using what we deem as wasted to produce beauty. What we see as meaningless is made meaningful in his love.

Will you come to God with the confidence of a dearly loved child today? He welcomes you with open arms, and he longs to speak his words of life over you. Take some time to listen to what he is saying. He will silence the lies with his truth. He will calm the chaos of uncertainty with his peace. He will love you to life again if you let him.

Thank the Father for his love.

Overcomers

"I have said these things to you, that in me you may have peace. In the world you will have tribulation. But take heart; I have overcome the world."

JOHN 16:33 ESV

Jesus does not expect us to turn a blind eye to our daily struggles. He knows that we will face trials and experience suffering. He acknowledges that we will walk through seasons of pain, grief, or even persecution. His acknowledgement of these things empowers us to face them without bitterness or offense.

When something difficult happens, you can approach the situation with confidence. Remember that Jesus has warned you and equipped you. He told you there would be trials, and he has given you everything you need to face them. He reminds you that you are strong because he is strong. His victory is your victory.

In the face of troubles, take heart! Jesus has already overcome them.

He Is Good

Give thanks to the LORD, for he is good
his love endures forever.

1 CHRONICLES 16:34 NIV

God's love for us is unchanging, always good, and without limits. His love for us is eternal and perfect. As we take time to reflect on the goodness of his love, we will realize that he has shown us mercy and grace that we don't deserve. His love for us isn't based on our skills, abilities, or strengths. He is faithful all the time despite our shortcomings.

Take time today to focus on the goodness of God. Choosing to dwell on his love rather than the frustrations of life makes all the difference. Turn toward him in gratitude and allow his love to transform your heart. Give thanks to the Lord and lean on his faithfulness.

Where you see goodness in your life, give thanks to God.

Childlike Faith

Jesus called for the children, saying, "Let the little children come to me. Don't stop them, because the kingdom of God belongs to people who are like these children."

LUKE 18:16 NCV

Jesus asks us to emulate children because their faith is pure and humble. Children are fully aware of their limitations, they know they have more to learn, and they hold fast to what they know is true. If we want to embrace childlike faith, we must be willing to humbly acknowledge our position before the Lord.

It takes deliberate effort to maintain a childlike faith as you grow and mature. Depend on your Father for grace and mercy and he will keep your heart soft. Allow the Holy Spirit to search your heart and actively surrender pride at the foot of the cross. Embrace grace over harsh standards, simple faith over meticulous religion, and mercy over judgment.

Let go of cynicism and ask God for his perspective.

There He Is

"If two or three people come together in my name,
I am there with them."

MATTHEW 18:20 NIV

God is not excluded from our relationships. When we gather in his name, no matter where we are or what we are doing, he is there in the fellowship. There is encouragement, power, and life in community. May we not forget the importance of fellowship for our whole health. Our souls, spirits, and bodies are refreshed and revived in the company of loving friendship.

You are not meant to live isolated from others. You were made to thrive in relationships. Think of the last time you had a really good conversation with a loved one. Did it not encourage your soul? Was it not refreshing to your heart? Do you see the importance of relating to others in authenticity and love? It is an invitation to deeper awareness, greater compassion, and shared joy.

Meet with a friend to pray and catch up.

Sought After

"The Son of Man has come to seek and to save that which was lost."

LUKE 19:10 NKJV

No matter how far we feel we have strayed, God is undeterred in his love toward us. He is the Shepherd who leaves the masses to seek out the one lost, vulnerable lamb. He does not give up on those he loves, so we cannot disqualify ourselves based on our own ideas of worthiness. After all, he turns coal to diamonds.

Jesus Christ is the same yesterday, today, and forever. He is not going to cast away the worn out or the defenseless. He goes to the edges of society and speaks his life over them. He is not too holy to show up in the most unexpected of places. Wherever you are, know that God pursues you with his fiery love. Turn to him, for he is near.

Recognize that no matter where you are today, you are not out of God's reach.

Endless Possibilities

Jesus looked at them and said to them, "With men this is impossible, but with God all things are possible."

MATTHEW 19:26 NKJV

Nothing is impossible for God. No matter how many limitations you experience, God has none. He is able to do far more than you could ever imagine asking him to do. He is able to save, redeem, and restore. With God, all things are possible.

Are there any areas of your life that feel unbearable? Are there any struggles that you just can't seem to shake? Look to the God who calms raging seas. The same God will calm the intense fear inside of you with his perfect peace. Pray to him, laying your heart bare before him. He is faithful and true, and he will not fail to meet you with his tangible mercy. Don't despair, for his resources are endless.

Thank God for his ability to do the impossible.

Run to Him

My God is my rock.
I can run to him for safety.
The LORD saves me from those who want to harm me.

2 SAMUEL 22:3 NCV

God is faithful and strong in times of trouble. He is our refuge, shield, and strong tower. He provides us with a constant source of protection and security. Our hearts will not be shaken when we have an accurate understanding of his character. Our confidence will not break when we trust in his unwavering presence and unfailing love.

When you truly grasp the magnitude of God's love and protection, gratitude will naturally fill your heart. How can you hold on to stress, anxiety, or negativity toward others when you are overwhelmed by the greatness of God's mercy toward you? He is your safety, and he provides you with everything you need.

Thank God for being your safe place.

Acknowledge Him

"Is not the LORD your God with you? And has He not given you rest on every side? For He has given the inhabitants of the land into my hand, and the land is subdued before the LORD and before His people."

1 CHRONICLES 22:19 NKJV

God's work in our lives begins with our intentional focus on him. He responds to us faithfully when we wholeheartedly look to him. We devote our lives to him, and he does not turn us away. We cannot expect him to move in our lives if we are unwilling to acknowledge who he is or what he has done for us.

There is power in deliberately praising God for his mighty works in your life. He has been with you for all your days. He has pursued you and drawn you close to his heart. He has intervened on your behalf, and he has sustained you. He has directed your steps and cleared your path. He alone is worthy of your praise.

Make a list of what God has done for you.

Upside-down Kingdom

"Who is the greater, one who reclines at table or one who serves? Is it not the one who reclines at table? But I am among you as the one who serves."

Luke 22:27 ESV

In a world where the greater your name is, the more pampered you are, it is refreshing to know that Jesus, the King of all creation, came to serve. He is the pinnacle of servant leadership, laying down his life so that we could know the extent of the Father's love. He is the living example of God's love.

May we never forget the importance of reaching out to others in love. As we look for opportunities to serve each other in both little and large ways, we become reflections of Jesus' glorious light. Where pride inflates our sense of importance, humility keeps us close to Jesus. Let's be like him in how we assist one another.

Look for ways to serve someone today.

Our Response

This God—his way is perfect;
the word of the LORD proves true;
he is a shield for all those who take refuge in him.

2 SAMUEL 22:31 ESV

God is our strength and shield. He protects us when we take refuge in him. His protection is contingent on our response to his faithfulness. We can't expect him to shelter us if we don't run to him when it storms. We can't expect him to move on our behalf if we never call upon his name. Our knowledge of God's perfection must translate into an intentional relationship with him.

God offers you the abundance of his perfection. His hands are open, and he longs for you to experience the blessing of his love and care. He doesn't expect you to wander through life alone or fight your own battles. Trust him with your life and he will equip you to face whatever comes your way. Offer him your heart and he will not disappoint you.

How can you deliberately turn to God today?

Always Faithful

"God is not man, that he should lie, or a son of man, that he should change his mind. Has he said, and will he not do it? Or has he spoken, and will he not fulfill it?"

Numbers 23:19 ESV

God's faithfulness is unwavering. He does not lie, change his mind, or leave his promises half fulfilled. His Word is reliable, and everything he does lines up with his character. He has proven himself trustworthy in every way. No matter what happens around us, we can remain steadfast because we know that God will keep his word.

Disappointments, unexpected grief, and broken promises can easily lead to bitterness, cynicism, and doubt. It's painful to keep your heart soft in the midst of suffering. Even so, it is worth it. As you refuse to let go of God's promises, he will strengthen your resolve. As you set your face like flint and cling to the Word, he will hold you up when you are too weak to stand.

Speak God's promises over your doubt.

Opened Understanding

Then he opened their minds to understand the Scriptures.

Luke 24:45 ESV

Without the help of God, can we really understand the vast goodness of his wisdom? We love because he first loved us. We believe him because he births faith within us. We are connected to him because he reached out to us to draw us to himself.

Is there a question that you have been wrestling with? Is there a problem you have not been able to solve? Ask the Lord to illuminate your understanding. What once was clouded becomes clear. There is nothing that we cannot ask God to help us with. May we press in even further, asking him to speak directly to us through his Word.

Before you read the Scriptures today, ask God to open your mind to his wisdom.

Wonderful Things

LORD, you are my God;
I will exalt you and praise your name,
for in perfect faithfulness
you have done wonderful things,
things planned long ago.

ISAIAH 25:1 NIV

Today's Scripture outlines a true act of worship. True worship consists of recognizing God's perfection and faithfulness and praising him for all he's done. Our hearts are transformed when we see God rightly and respond with devotion. As we exalt his name, he reminds us of his faithfulness and strengthens us in our weakness. He doesn't ask us to worship him out of obligation or because his ego demands it. He knows that through worship our eyes are opened to his goodness and love.

If you are struggling through something right now, turn to the Lord worship. Set aside a deliberate time to praise him. Look to him and acknowledge his faithfulness. Let the goodness of his presence fill you with peace and hope. Expect him to transform your heart because he will.

Praise God for his fulfilled promises in your life.

Reliable Defense

You have been a stronghold for the helpless,
A stronghold for the poor in his distress,
A refuge from the storm, a shade from the heat;
For the breath of the ruthless
Is like a rain storm against a wall.

Isaiah 25:4 NASB

Whatever trouble we are facing, we can take it to the Lord. Whatever distress we are feeling, he can handle every bit of it. He is not overwhelmed by our messy emotions. He welcomes us as we are, and he covers us in the cloak of his loving kindness. We can press into the safety of his presence, for he is our protector and place of rest. We can run to him whenever we feel unsure.

How has God been a shelter for you in times of trouble? Have you seen his hand of protection over your life in specific instances? Even if you cannot pinpoint one in this moment, let your mind meditate on his sovereignty. God is unflappable. He is unshakable. He is full of loyal love, and he guards his children like a good shepherd guards his flock.

Write down how God has defended you and kept you safe.

Peace of Mind

You keep him in perfect peace
whose mind is stayed on you,
because he trusts in you.

Isaiah 26:3 ESV

We are all prone to different expressions of anxiety. Some of us worry about money, while some of us are hyper-aware of our relationships. Some of us are terrified of health issues, while others worry about their position in their career. No matter how fear is expressed in your life, there is no need to be bound to it. Jesus offers you steady and persistent peace.

Turn your thoughts to Jesus whenever you feel the talons of anxiety clawing at you. Look to him, meditate on his Word, and remember his faithfulness. Take heart because he is nearer than you know! When you don't know what else to do, let the prayers of your heart connect you to the Spirit of God. He will keep you in perfect peace when you turn your attention toward him.

Keep bringing your thoughts back to God's faithfulness throughout your day.

The Everlasting Way

Search me, God, and know my heart;
test me and know my anxious thoughts.
See if there is any offensive way in me,
and lead me in the way everlasting.

Psalm 139:23-24 NIV

The Lord knows us completely. When we invite his wisdom and leadership into our lives, we open ourselves up to his lifegiving words. He course-corrects those who look to him. No matter how lost we may feel, God is never at a loss. He always sees a way out, provides clarity for our confusion, and redirects us as we take hold of his hand.

Today is the perfect opportunity to invite God to search your heart. As he tests you and sees your anxious thoughts, he can speak life and correction to you. When you look at your problems in the light of his presence, what was cloudy becomes clear. You can trust God to lead you toward everlasting life again and again.

Invite the Lord to search your heart and redirect you in his love.

Do the Work

"Be strong and courageous, and do the work. Don't be afraid or discouraged, for the LORD God, my God, is with you. He will not fail you or forsake you. He will see to it that all the work related to the Temple of the LORD is finished."

1 CHRONICLES 28:20 NLT

Whatever work we have to do, we can do it unto the Lord. He has not called us to live a life that is disconnected from responsibilities or reality. In each of our tasks, God is present. When he leads us, he provides all the strength we need. He does not leave us alone to navigate the path he lays out for us.

Everything that you do for the Lord matters. Every act of courage, faith, and strength is worthwhile. He sees it all, and you can trust him to be by your side. He won't ever abandon you or leave you alone to struggle. You can rely on his leadership, and he will take care of the details you cannot.

Put energy into your work with a thankful heart, knowing God is with you in it.

Constant Companionship

"I am with you always, to the end of the age."

MATTHEW 28:20 NASB

The promise of Jesus' presence is powerful. We are never alone no matter where we go, what we do, or what struggles we encounter. When our faith feels weak and we don't think we have what it takes, we can depend on him. When we are filled with doubt and cannot take another step, he has not forgotten us. When our perseverance is dwindling and we feel hopeless, he is with us.

You are strong because Jesus is with you. You can endure because he will not let you fall. You might stumble and you might grow weary, but with his help you will surely make it to the end of your race. You will cross the finish line not because you trained or you willed it into existence, but because he has been with you every step of the way.

Thank God for his presence that never leaves.

Only a Moment

We are here for only a moment, visitors and strangers in the land as our ancestors were before us. Our days on earth are like a passing shadow, gone so soon without a trace.

1 Chronicles 29:15 NLT

This life is fleeting. Though we may live through seasons that seem to drag on, the truth of the matter is that we are only passing through like travelers in a strange land. May we embrace the time we have and use every opportunity to choose to live with love, kindness, and purpose.

What is your underlying motivation? What vision are you moving toward? What values drive you? Take time to sift out unhelpful habits that don't serve you or others well and keep those you want to prioritize. You only have one precious life. How do you want to be known by those closest to you? What do you want your legacy to be? Take the opportunity you have today to choose how you will live.

Deliberately decide what kind of life you want to have.

All Is His

"Lord our God, all this abundance that we have provided to build You a house for Your holy name, it is from Your hand, and everything is Yours."

1 Chronicles 29:16 NASB

May we approach God with hearts that are full of gratitude. May we have a revelation of the goodness of God, recognizing all he has done for us. There is nothing in this world that remains outside the realm of his merciful kindness. He has filled our lives with incredible gifts, and we can offer him our hearts in return.

There is power in the practice of open-handed generosity. When you sense a desire to hoard his blessings, may you turn to the Lord and give him access to your heart. Ask him for a fresh revelation of the vastness of his kingdom. Remember that none of his resources are limited, and you can share with others because he will faithfully provide for you. As you stay humble in his love, generosity will flow from a place of devotion and trust.

Give back to God a portion of what you have, thanking him for his generosity.

Compassionate and Kind

The Lord longs to be gracious to you;
therefore he will rise up to show you compassion.
For the Lord is a God of justice.
Blessed are all who wait for him!

Isaiah 30:18 NIV

While God certainly uses suffering to draw us closer to him, it's important to understand that he is not the author of pain in our lives. He longs to be gracious to us. He wants us to experience goodness, love, peace, and contentment. His intentions toward us are perfect and pure. He is capable of using hardship for his glory and our good, but bitterness will grow in our hearts if we don't recognize the distinction between creating pain and equipping us to manage it.

God longs to be gracious to you. Let the truth of that statement sink deep into your heart. Do you believe it? Or are you waiting for the other shoe to drop? Does your mind constantly conjure up worst case scenarios, or do you always assume that God is preparing a treacherous path for you to navigate? How might your outlook change if you were convinced of God's goodness and compassion?

Ask God to soften your heart.

Listen and Trust

Your ears shall hear a word behind you, saying,
"This is the way, walk in it,"
Whenever you turn to the right hand
or whenever you turn to the left."

ISAIAH 30:21 NKJV

God is more involved in our lives than we can know. When we ask him to direct our choices, he will lead us in wisdom. When we come to the proverbial fork in the road, he will guide us when we listen for his voice. We need not rely solely on our own logic; we can also lean on the wonderful leadership of the Spirit with us.

What would it look like to practice hearing the voice of the Lord in your decision-making? The Spirit knows you so well. When you ask for the Lord's input, you can trust that he knows what's best. He sees your entire life clearly, and he is capable of leading you through it.

Ask God to direct your choices today.

No Wrong

He is the Rock, his works are perfect, and all his ways are just. A faithful God who does no wrong, upright and just is he.

DEUTERONOMY 32:4 NIV

Our hearts are protected when we are convinced of the goodness of God's character. Everything he does is right and just. His motives are always pure, and he is always faithful. He keeps his promises, and his judgment is perfect. Even when we don't understand a particular situation, we don't give in to fear or doubt because we know God is sovereign.

Lies don't phase you when you are convinced of the truth. If you know something deep in your heart, it doesn't matter what anyone else might say. Strive for this to be the case with your trust in God. The world might hurl accusations at him and the people around you might waver, but by his grace and mercy you can stand strong. Look to him daily and ask him to strengthen your resolve.

What truths about God are you absolutely convinced of?

Never Lost

He found them in a desert,
a windy, empty land.
He surrounded them and brought them up,
guarding them as those he loved very much.

Deuteronomy 32:10 NCV

No matter where we find ourselves in this life, we are never out of God's sight. He sees us, and he knows exactly where we are even if we are unable to discern it for ourselves. He surrounds us with his kindness, and he guards us with his mercy. When we are in the desert, surrounded by barrenness, may we sense the nearness of our Good Shepherd.

Have you felt lost lately? Perhaps you are out of the wilderness, but you vividly remember what it felt like. Look to God today and remember his faithfulness. He has not left you yet, and he never will. May his Spirit remind you of the deposits of his kindness that have sustained you along your journey so far. He is still leading you in his compassion even now.

Write a poem of thanks to God for his protection.

Safe and Secure

"My people will live in safety, quietly at home.
They will be at rest."

ISAIAH 32:18 TPT

We can find our peaceful home in Christ. We can experience the rest of his presence at all times. We can lay our worries down and put our trust in him. In the fellowship of the Spirit, we experience the overwhelming peace of his nearness. He is eager to comfort us and quiet our souls.

Whatever troubles you have been facing, may you know that you are safe and secure in the love of God. He is your refuge and your sustenance. He is full of refreshing springs to revive your weary heart. He does not leave you to be overwhelmed by your circumstances. He is with you in every trial and every storm. He is as confident and sure in your darkest night as he is on your brightest day. May you find deep rest for your soul in his presence.

Remember a time when God gave you peace to calm your storms.

Make Him Known

Oh, give thanks to the Lord!
Call upon His name;
Make known His deeds among the peoples!

1 Chronicles 16:8 NKJV

Our testimony is an account of where we have seen God move in our lives. It's the story of how he has met us with his love and transformed what we could never change on our own. Everyone has a unique story to tell, and God is glorified when we acknowledge how he has moved in both simple and elaborate ways.

Think back over your walk with God and ask him for his perspective. Ask him to remind you of how he has moved on your behalf. There is power in remembrance, and there is power in the word of your testimony. Whenever the opportunity arises, share what God has done for you. As you do, you may find that your faith grows as you recall God's goodness.

Share a testimony of gratitude with someone today.

April

Praise the Lord.
Give thanks to the Lord, for he is good;
his love endures forever.

Psalm 106:1 NIV

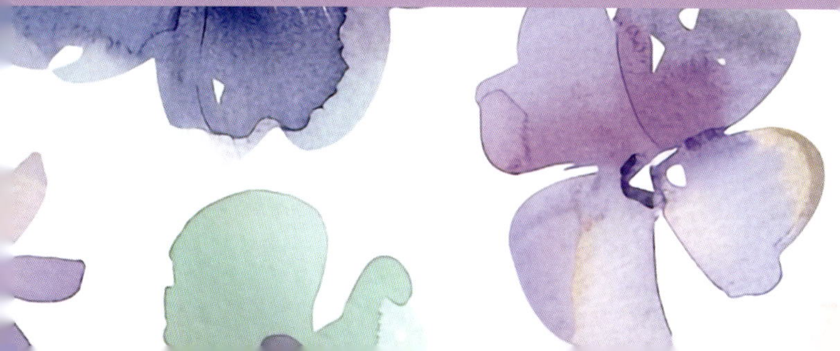

Good and Pleasing

Don't copy the behavior and customs of this world, but let God transform you into a new person by changing the way you think. Then you will learn to know God's will for you, which is good and pleasing and perfect.

Romans 12:2 NLT

When we prioritize God's ways over the world's ways, we will experience the joy of knowing we are walking according to his will. He gently shows us what is right, and he gives us the tools we need to live according to his standards. As we honor him with our choices, we will see that his will for our lives is good, pleasing, and perfect.

There will be times when you would rather follow the world or your own flesh. There will be times when it seems more comfortable, satisfying, or immediately rewarding to do something that is outside of God's will. When this happens, it can be helpful to remember that God's ways really are best. His plan for your life is not arbitrary. He has called you to live a certain way because he knows what will bring you true joy, peace, and eternal life.

Ask God for perseverance.

God Alone

The eternal God is your refuge.

Deuteronomy 33:27 NIV

A consistent message within modern culture is the importance of safety and well-being. We are constantly being told to create and seek safe spaces. While it's not inherently wrong to desire feelings of acceptance and peace, it's important to recognize that God is our only true source. If we look for refuge in cultural patterns or the acceptance of others, we will always come up short.

God alone is your refuge. He is the only one who cannot be shaken, changed, or overcome. He will not let you down, and you can depend on him for peace. All other sources of peace are temporary and will not last. When you look for validation from him rather than other people, you will not be disappointed.

Give God your worries.

At All Times

I will praise the Lord at all times;
his praise is always on my lips.

Psalm 34:1 NCV

In all things, at all times, there is always a reason to offer praise to the Living God. Praise him, for his mercies never end! Praise him, for he meets us with the power of his love in overwhelming measure when we look to him. Praise him, for he is with us even in our deepest pain and suffering.

May praises rise from your heart in an unending stream of thanksgiving. Cultivate gratitude by practicing saying thank you. Thank him for his constant presence. Thank him for his clarifying wisdom. Thank him for the sun on your face and the food on your table. No detail is too small. No offering of praise is insignificant. It all counts, and he recognizes each one. Let all that is within you offer grateful praise to your God and King.

Praise God throughout your day, giving him thanks for who he is and what he has done.

Perfect Character

"The Lord, the Lord, the compassionate and gracious God, slow to anger, abounding in love and faithfulness."

Exodus 34:6 NIV

Some of us grew up with kind and patient parents, and some of us did not. Some of us are used to the idea of authority figures being responsible and compassionate, and some of us can't quite wrap our heads around the concept. God in all of his might, power, and authority, is infinitely kind. He is compassionate, gracious, and slow to anger. Every part of him is good, loving, and faithful.

Let your ideas of authority be challenged by the perfect nature of God. If you are unfamiliar with gentle leadership, allow God to soften your heart. If you are baffled by his patience, let him surprise you with his long-suffering mercy. Thank God for the beauty of his grace and compassion and ask him to reveal it to you even more.

Ask God to give you insight into your understanding of his character.

He Is Strong

Say to those with fearful hearts,
"Be strong, and do not fear,
for your God...is coming to save you."

Isaiah 35:4 NLT

Fear can make people do irrational things. When there is fear in our hearts we might make faithless decisions, treat others less than kindly, or live as slaves to anxiety. None of these behaviors capture God's intention for our lives. He longs for us to know the all-encompassing peace that comes from knowing he is on our side.

When you allow fear to dictate how you live, you will miss out on God's best for you. He doesn't want you to be afraid of worst-case scenarios, and he doesn't expect you to foresee every possible negative scenario. Instead, he offers you peace. He gently reminds you that he is in control, and he will not let you down. Pay attention to the feeling of fear and notice how you react to it.

Write down your fears. Ask God to speak his truth over them.

Good Shepherd

He takes care of his people like a shepherd.
He gathers them like lambs in his arms
and carries them close to him.
He gently leads the mothers of the lambs.

Isaiah 40:11 NCV

God cares for us like a shepherd cares for his sheep. He is attentive toward us, and he knows what we need. A good shepherd knows the weaknesses in his flock, and he compensates for them. He knows that mothers of lambs need extra help, and he faithfully provides it. In the same way, God knows our weaknesses and faithfully equips us to persevere or overcome.

God knows exactly what season of life you are in. He knows what you need to accomplish the tasks in front of you each day. He knows your weaknesses, and he knows the challenges you will face before you see them coming. Today, thank him for his expert care and look for evidence of his compassion toward you. Pay attention to his provision and allow your heart to shift from frustration to gratitude.

Thank God for his gentle leadership in your life.

Each Star

Raise your eyes on high
And see who has created these stars,
The One who brings out their multitude by number,
He calls them all by name.

Isaiah 40:26 NASB

We serve a God who is unlike any other. He alone has created everything we see with intention and incredible precision. He knit each corner of creation together, and he sustains all of it. His wisdom, power, and might are displayed by the mysteries of our world and the universe that contains it. He knows how each piece interacts with every other part. He does not forget one single part of his creation.

You are seen by the God who sees everything and everyone. If he keeps track of the stars, surely he keeps track of you. He knows when you are happy, and he knows when you are suffering. He is aware of every part of your life, and he has what you need in every season. You are not too much for him. Allow him to orchestrate your life in the same way he orchestrates the heavens.

Go outside tonight and look at the stars, remembering their Creator is yours too.

He Doesn't Tire

"Do you not know? Have you not heard? The Lord is the everlasting God, the Creator of the ends of the earth. He will not grow tired or weary, and his understanding no one can fathom."

Isaiah 40:28 NIV

In our mortal bodies, it is difficult to imagine never growing tired. We work, eat, sleep, then begin again the next day. Without enough water, food, or rest, we do not function well. We were created for rhythms of restoration, and that includes feeding our bodies, minds, and souls. God, however, is the fullness of life. He never grows tired or irritable.

May you find encouragement in the strength of the Lord instead of finding shame in your weakness. The Lord is your Creator, and he is well aware of your limits. He didn't create you to burn out by never resting. Lean on his strength and rest in his perfection.

In your weariness, realize that God is great, and he never tires of helping you.

Opportunity for Strength

He gives strength to those who are tired
and more power to those who are weak.

Isaiah 40:29 NCV

There has never been, nor will there ever be, a time when God holds our weaknesses over our heads. He is not a God who exploits our limitations or shames us when we don't measure up. When we are weak, he is strong. When we are tired, his power is magnified. Weakness is not a negative thing. It's an opportunity to worship God who is without weakness of any kind.

You get to choose your reaction to your own weaknesses. You can choose shame, embarrassment, or anger. You can also choose to humbly give your weaknesses to God with confidence, knowing that he can use them for his glory. There is no need to be brutal toward your flaws when God is willing to strengthen you. No matter what your struggle looks like, God has what you need.

Thank God for the opportunity to turn to him in weakness.

No Room

Those who hope in the LORD
will renew their strength.
They will soar on wings like eagles;
they will run and not grow weary,
they will walk and not be faint.

ISAIAH 40:31 NIV

When we focus on the blessings in our lives, we can displace bitterness, anger, and resentment with peace, joy, and compassion. One of those blessings is that God is always with us, and he is our source of life. When we focus on who he is and how he provides for us, we make space for the fruit of his kingdom to be abundantly present in our lives.

God offers you abundant life. He offers you strength, perseverance, and hope. When these things are the defining factors of your life, there isn't room for resentment or fear. Anger and bitterness are diminished by standing firmly on the truth of who God is. Rather than focusing on the things you lack, turn your eyes toward him today and allow him to fill your heart with confident trust in who he is.

How has focusing on God changed your attitude in the past?

Held Up

Don't be afraid, for I am with you.
Don't be discouraged, for I am your God.
I will strengthen you and help you.
I will hold you up with my victorious right hand.

Isaiah 41:10 NLT

God is on our side. He is loyal to his people, and he is attentive to our cries. He hears us when we call upon his name, and he is always ready to intervene on our behalf. While we aren't promised a life without suffering or grief, we are promised the faithful presence of God no matter what is going on in our lives.

In your discouragement, do not give way to despair. In your disappointment, do not forget who God is. He is loyal in love, and he restores all things. He is a helper to the needy, and he gives strength to the weak. He upholds those whose knees buckle under the weight of worry. Give him your heavy burdens. He can handle them, and he knows exactly what you need.

Remember a time when God helped you and thank him for it.

Unstoppable

"I know that you can do anything,
and no one can stop you."

Job 42:2 NLT

We all have areas of our lives where our weaknesses are magnified. While the details look different for everyone, we all have sins or habits we struggle with. Our ability to bring our sins to God matters more than the sins themselves. He has given us victory over sin and death. Through Jesus, we have freedom from the chains that used to bind us.

Don't forget the incredible miracle of the gospel. You have been set free and made new. You have access to the same power that rose Christ from the dead. You have victory in all things! Don't give in to the lie that you cannot change or will always be stuck in the same patterns and habits. God can do anything, and your struggles are not beyond his ability to help you.

Surrender the impossible situations in your life to God.

Redeemed by Love

"I have redeemed you;
I have called you by name;
you are Mine!"

Isaiah 43:1 NASB

Where we find our identity will affect how we live. When we know who we belong to and where we come from, we can own the power of our heritage. It doesn't matter what our earthly family looks like. When we come to Jesus, he welcomes us into his family.

When you yield your life to Christ, you find your identity in who he says you are. You can let go of any other defining factors and settle into the comfort and security of his kingdom. You are loved, wanted, accepted, and pursued. The Most High has called you by name and declared that you belong to him. Allow his love for you to take up all the space in your heart, leaving no room for comparison, competition, or hatred of your brother.

How does understanding your true identity impact the way you treat others?

In Control

"Even from eternity I am He,
And there is no one who can rescue from My hand;
I act, and who can reverse it?"

Isaiah 43:13 NASB

There is freedom to be found in releasing the tight grasp we have on our lives. There is peace to be realized in recognizing that God alone is in control. He accomplishes his will, and no one can reverse it. We don't have to worry about his authority because he moves with compassion, wisdom, and love. He joyfully and faithfully intervenes on behalf of his people.

You do not serve a God who sits idly by. He calls you by name, and he holds you close. He moves at the sound of your voice, and he longs for you to know his faithfulness. You can trust him with the details of your life because he has proven himself faithful. He has watched over his people from the beginning of time, and he will mindfully watch over you.

How have you experienced God's mindfulness?

In the Wilderness

"I am about to do something new.
See, I have already begun! Do you not see it?
I will make a pathway through the wilderness.
I will create rivers in the dry wasteland."

Isaiah 43:19 NLT

There is never a time when we are left alone to struggle through life. There is never a season when God withholds his presence or refuses to empower us with mercy and grace. Even when we find ourselves in the wilderness or on an unexpected path, God is faithful to lead us.

When your circumstances are challenging, God is with you. When you can't see a way through the trial you are facing, God is with you. When it seems impossible to take another step, God is with you. He is capable and willing to make a way when you cannot find one. When you reach the end of your abilities, God can create pathways that lead to life and renewal.

How have you seen God operate in impossible situations?

Swept Away

"I have swept away offences like a cloud,
your sins like the morning mist.
Return to me, for I have redeemed you."

Isaiah 44:22 NIV

We aren't walking in the freedom Christ offers us when we hold onto guilt and shame. There is no reason to punish or berate ourselves for our past mistakes. While we might still experience some of the natural consequences of our actions, God has declared us free and redeemed. In his eyes, our offenses are nonexistent.

Unnecessary guilt can impact every part of your life. It can cause you to treat other people with the same judgment you expect for yourself. It can cause you to hold onto mistakes and failures even when God has declared you are free. Remind yourself as often as needed that God has swept away your offences. Speak truth over yourself until you believe it fully.

How has personal guilt impacted the way you treat others?

Hidden Treasures

"I will give you hidden treasures,
riches stored in secret places,
so that you may know that I am the LORD,
the God of Israel, who summons you by name."

ISAIAH 45:3 NIV

God longs for us to know him. His desire is that we would have uninterrupted fellowship with him. He is not hiding from us, and he is not far away. He has made himself fully available to us through Christ. He pursues us consistently, and he offers us as much knowledge of his heart and character as we want.

If you want to be closer to God, there is nothing standing in your way. You get to have as close of a relationship with him as you want. He will never limit your pursuit of him, and he will never withhold his presence. When you seek him, you will find him. When you devote your life to knowing him, you won't be disappointed.

Seek the Lord with confidence, knowing that he will respond.

Relief in Him

Sing for joy. For the Lord has comforted his people and will have compassion on them in their suffering.

Isaiah 49:13 NLT

When we are burdened by the hardness of life, God is our comfort. When unexpected tragedies lead us into deep grief, God is with us in the pain and suffering. Jesus knows what it is like to suffer. He was a man of many sorrows, handed over to those who wanted his life for a few silver coins. He knows what suffering is because he lived it himself.

The Spirit of God is your very present help in times of trouble. He is your very near comfort in times of mourning. He is with you. He gives you relief in his presence. He mourns with you, holds you close, and speaks tenderly to your heart. There is no need to rush into feeling better. Hold onto him and take the time and space you need to grieve your losses.

Thank God for his nearness in suffering.

Deliberate Trust

The Lord God helps Me,
Therefore, I am not disgraced;
Therefore, I have made My face like flint,
And I know that I will not be ashamed.

ISAIAH 50:7 NASB

Our peace is quickly disturbed when we allow ourselves to be blown about by the troubles of this life. When our stability depends on our circumstances we will quickly realize that we are in desperate need of an anchor that will hold fast in any storm. God is our steady and reliable anchor. We must deliberately choose to trust him even when our situation seems impossible.

There is a confidence that settles deep in your soul when you know God is defending, helping, and walking alongside you. This confidence allows you to be unshaken and unbothered when trials arise. You can put one foot in front of the other no matter what comes your way because you know that God is for you.

Trust what God has said and walk confidently in his steps.

Heart of Surrender

My sacrifice, O God, is a broken spirit;
a broken and contrite heart you, God,
will not despise.

Psalm 51:17 NIV

Gratitude often begins with brokenness. When we come to God with a humble heart, fully aware of our failures and weaknesses, he doesn't turn us away. He welcomes us when we are at our worst, and he faithfully transforms our hearts in his presence. We surrender, he rescues us, and we respond in turn with gratitude and thanksgiving.

Pursuing brokenness of spirit doesn't sound very appealing. It's not comfortable, and your flesh will likely scream in resistance. We don't naturally want to admit our faults or bear our open wounds. Remember that brokenness and humility are signs of true strength. You are the strongest when you offer your contrite heart to the Lord.

Offer Jesus access to your heart today.

Finished

I will praise you forever for what you have done.
In the presence of your faithful people,
I will put my hope in your name, for it is good.

Psalm 52:9 CSB

Christ has done everything necessary to clear the way to the Father. The finished work of the cross is all we need to look to. He is the door, and all who enter through relationship with him find themselves in the fullness of God's mercy. There is nothing to add to what he has already accomplished, and there is nothing that can take away from the power of his resurrection life.

Today, lay aside everything that has kept you from coming to Jesus. Can you give him your full attention for a few minutes? You don't need to get your emotions under control or feel full of faith to approach him. He is full of loyal love toward you right now, and he welcomes you with the generosity of his gracious heart.

Give God a few minutes of undistracted time today.

Unfailing Love

"Though the mountains be shaken and the hills be removed, yet my unfailing love for you will not be shaken nor my covenant of peace be removed," says the LORD, who has compassion on you.

ISAIAH 54:10 NIV

When God makes a covenant, he never goes back on it. His covenant through Christ is a forever promise. It is a vow that he will keep. His compassion is evident through the life, ministry, and sacrifice of Christ. His power is made clear through the resurrection of his body from the grave. There is nothing that can keep his unfailing love from meeting us where we are.

Don't despair, for the fullness of Christ's mercy and kindness are yours today and forever. Even when everything that can be shaken in this world is quaking, the love of the Lord remains unshakable. He is as steadfast in mercy in this moment as he ever has been or ever will be. He will always keep his promises.

Thank God for his reliable and faithful love that is always available through Jesus.

So Much Joy

You will go out with joy and be led out in peace.
The mountains and hills will burst into song before you,
and all the trees in the fields will clap their hands.

Isaiah 55:12 NCV

God's promises don't just offer us contentment, they are overflowing with joy and peace. We get to partake in a vibrant creation-wide celebration of God's goodness. We are part of a glorious story that depicts God's steady faithfulness and will culminate in the full expression of his glory on the day of his return. He will make all things right, and those of us who have endured to the end will celebrate for eternity.

The joy and peace that you can find through a relationship with the Lord cannot be compared to anything you can muster up yourself. There is nothing on this earth that will satisfy you like his presence. There is nothing you can devote your life to that will give you as much in return as surrendering your heart to the Lord. He is well worth the investment.

How can you celebrate your relationship with God today?

Gardens of Glory

The Lord will guide you always;
he will satisfy your needs in a sun-scorched land
and will strengthen your frame.
You will be like a well-watered garden,
like a spring whose waters never fail.

Isaiah 58:11 NIV

If we imagine a well-watered garden we might picture an abundance of life. We would see various plants thriving and bearing fruit. We'd see flowers blooming, bees buzzing, and birds chirping. From the roots deep in the healthy soil to the leaves blowing the soft breeze, everything works together and creates an environment that is nourished, fruitful, and beautiful.

When you devote your heart to the Lord and lean on him for guidance, you are like a well-watered garden. You are full of life and are overflowing with evidence of his goodness. He satisfies your needs and strengthens you when you are weak. You can have confidence because you know he will not fail you.

Commune with the Spirit, thanking God for his waters of refreshment.

Better Word

"I will give them a crown to replace their ashes, and the oil of gladness to replace their sorrow, and clothes of praise to replace their spirit of sadness."

Isaiah 61:3 NCV

Nowhere in the Word does God tell us to ignore our sadness. He does not instruct us to deny the pain and suffering we experience or gloss over the tragedies and losses of life. Our tendencies to push down our emotions don't line up with God's desire to comfort, encourage, and protect us. We were not created to strong arm our way through grief. We were created to lean on the Lord in the midst of it.

Oh, the wondrous beauty of God's kindness! He says that he will give you a crown of beauty to replace the ashes of your despair. He offers you the oil of his gladness which will seep into your sorrow and turn your mourning into joy. He gives you clothes of praise to replace the spirit of sadness. You will dance again! You will sing, and you will rise up in the glory of his healing presence. There is hope for the future, and there is peace for today.

When you feel sad, ask God to minister to you in it.

None Like Him

Since ancient times no one has heard,
no ear has perceived,
no eye has seen any God besides you,
who acts on behalf of those who wait for him.

Isaiah 64:4 NIV

There is no one like God who sent his own Son to show us the power of his kingdom ways. In Matthew 5, Jesus lays out the difference between what was understood about the laws of God and what the kingdom of heaven actually requires. But he did not stop there! Knowing that perfection was beyond any of us, he provided a way out from the shame and fear that kept us stuck.

In Christ's death and resurrection, you will find true life. All who come to the Father through Jesus are made new. If you surrender to him, you are made alive in the presence of his unfailing love. His ability to intervene on your behalf and redeem you is miraculous. He alone provides his people with salvation, fullness of life, and eternal glory.

Surrender to the miraculous work of God in your life.

Eternal Portion

My flesh and my heart fail;
But God is the strength of my heart
and my portion forever.

Psalm 73:26 NKJV

Even when our bodies fail us and our hearts grow weary, strength is still found in the living presence of God. He is the strength of our hearts, and he will always be our perfect portion. This does not mean that we will experience an easy life without flaws or pain. We are not promised a world without trouble, but we are promised the presence of God through it all.

May you know the peace of God that transcends your circumstances. May you know his nearness in your frailty and your losses. In all things, offer your body as a living sacrifice to the Lord. Let the power of God permeate your life through and through. He is your hope, strength, and deliverance.

How can you rely on God for strength over your own physical abilities today?

His People

Know that the LORD Himself is God;
It is He who has made us, and not we ourselves;
We are His people and the sheep of His pasture.

PSALM 100:3 NASB

When we remember who we are, gratitude naturally fills our hearts. We belong to God. We are his creation, and he calls us his people. We are the sheep of his pasture, and he loves taking care of us. He is not the kind of creator who makes something and then stores it away to be forgotten or moves along to his next masterpiece. Of everything God has made, we are his prized possession.

Thank God today for his attentive kindness. He created you with purpose and intention, and he has not forgotten you. Let your heart relax in his presence and allow a sense of belonging to fill your soul. You matter to him. He knows you inside and out, and he loves you perfectly. He sees every part of you, and he will not turn away from you.

How can you express gratitude to God today?

Always Good

The Lord is good.
His unfailing love continues forever,
and his faithfulness continues to each generation.

Psalm 100:5 NLT

When life is difficult, it is tempting to let bitterness take root. It feels momentarily satisfying to dwell on our frustrations and vent our anger. We want to be validated, heard, and justified. While it's not wrong to process through our circumstances and the emotions they stir up, it's important to consistently acknowledge God's goodness along the way.

The Lord is good no matter what. His unfailing love will never end. His goodness stretches beyond your failures and the wrongs you've endured. He has been faithful to every generation before you, and he will be faithful for all of your days. The truth of God's goodness can soften your heart and keep your perspective steady no matter what you are going through.

Allow God's goodness to shift your attitude and draw you closer to him.

Thankful for Rescue

Save us, Lord our God,
and gather us from the nations,
so that we may give thanks to your holy name
and rejoice in your praise.

Psalm 106:47 CSB

In Psalm 106 the psalmist cries out to the Lord for help. He knows that he needs the Lord to rescue him and that he is helpless without him. He is fully aware of his dependency on God, and he longs for God to intervene so that he can offer him heartfelt praise and genuine gratitude.

You can approach God the same way as the psalmist. When you remember what God has done for you and approach him with thanksgiving, you'll find it difficult to hold on to hatred or bitterness. When you face new problems and expect God to help you, you'll remain confident and steady with your eyes on him. There is no need to be thrown off course by the trials of life when God has gathered you with grace and mercifully brought you close to himself.

How can you increase your faith and expect God to save you when problems arise?

May

Rejoice always, pray continually, give thanks in all circumstance; for this is God's will for you in Christ Jesus.

1 Thessalonians 5:16-18 NIV

Mercy over Sacrifice

"Go and learn the meaning of this Scripture: 'I want you to show mercy, not offer sacrifices.' For I have come to call not those who think they are righteous, but those who know they are sinners."

MATTHEW 9:13 NLT

Christianity is not about what we can accomplish or how we can succeed. It's not about checking items off a list or making sure our lives look just right. Jesus calls us to value mercy above sacrifice. Matthew 9 reminds us that the state of our hearts is much more important than the outward appearance of righteousness. Jesus doesn't want obedience for the sake of obedience; he wants our humble and surrendered hearts.

When you value mercy over sacrifice you won't be shaken by your failures and weaknesses. When you have an accurate understanding of God's response to humility you won't hesitate to bare your soul before him. Knowing that he will cover you with his love and strengthen you when you are weak gives you the confidence to be honest, transparent, and open with him.

Share your weaknesses with the Lord.

Everyday Miracles

He causes us to remember his wonderful works.
How gracious and merciful is our LORD!

PSALM 111:4 NLT

It's easy to forget God's goodness when we get lost in the mundane details of our lives. Our vision gets clouded by our routines, schedules, and goals, and we lose sight of the many miracles God is constantly performing. He is always intervening on our behalf; we just have to take the time to notice it.

Your life is filled with evidence of God's goodness. He is constantly sustaining, protecting, and equipping you. If you have surrendered your life into his hands there isn't a single moment when you are without him. You don't have to search the earth for his glory or spend your life waiting for the next big miracle. Your very existence is evidence of God's love for you.

How have you seen God's grace at work lately?

Trustworthy Truth

All he does is just and good,
and all his commandments are trustworthy.

Psalm 111:7 NLT

God is always good. This is a truth that never fades or changes. Even when everything around us is crumbling, God's goodness remains. When hope seems lost and we cannot see a way out of our current predicament, his faithfulness hasn't failed. As we cling to his commandments, he will encourage us and give us strength.

Dwelling on the goodness of God is like a shield around your heart. As you focus on who he is and all he's done, you'll be protected from bitterness and doubt. The struggles of life seem less harsh when your eyes are turned toward him. When you lean upon his promises instead of your physical circumstances, he will give you perseverance to face whatever comes your way.

Yield your heart in trust to Jesus and his ways today.

His Choice

"No one takes it from me, but I lay it down of my own accord. I have authority to lay it down, and I have authority to take it up again. This charge I have received from my Father."

JOHN 10:8 ESV

Life does not simply happen to us. In any moment, we are able to choose how we will respond. We get to choose the mindsets that we live by. We get to choose to rely on God's faithfulness. He is long-lasting in loyal love. Jesus, when coming to this earth, chose to live out the Father's love. He chose to partner with mercy and show us the way to the kingdom of God.

Though we cannot control what will happen in this life, we do choose our reactions and responses. We get to take ownership of the attitude of our hearts. We get to choose who we turn to for help when we need it. Will we remain dependent on Jesus? Will we trust him to do what we cannot? Will we rely on his faithfulness more than our own? He is good. He is better than any other. Whatever we choose, let's own it today.

Take ownership of your choices today.

Day of Rejoicing

This is the day which the Lord has made;
Let us rejoice and be glad in it.

Psalm 118:24 NASB

Today is the only thing we can grasp hold of. Yesterday is in the past; the future is still out of reach. Today we get to decide how we will spend our time, where we will focus our thoughts, and what kind of attitude we'll display. Today is a gift, and we get to decide how we will use it.

May you find a reason to rejoice. Maybe it's the simple pleasure of your morning cup of coffee, the way the light filters through your window, or the fresh air that greets your lungs as you step outside. May you find peace in the presence of the Lord. May you find reason after reason to give thanks until it is a steady rhythm that overflows from your soul onto your lips.

Look for reasons to give thanks throughout your day.

Revived in Hope

Your promise revives me;
it comforts me in all my troubles.

Psalm 119:50 NLT

There is hope to be found in the promises of the Lord. He is faithful in all he does, and we can trust him to follow through on his word. We can build our lives upon his promises, and we can rest securely, knowing that he won't let us down.

Take some time to pray, inviting the Spirit of peace to settle over your heart and mind as you give him all your worries and cares. Let the comfort of the Lord meet you no matter what your troubles are. May hope rise up within you as he speaks his words of life over you.

Spend time in prayer and thank God for his faithfulness.

Loving Wisdom

Give thanks to the Creator
who made the heavens with wisdom!
His tender love for us continues on forever!

Psalm 136:5 TPT

The loving wisdom of the Lord guides us through the challenges of this life. When we look to his leadership, we will find his solutions are our portion. He used wisdom to create the heavens, and he uses wisdom to guide us through each of our days.

When you are not sure how to move forward, look to the Lord for direction. He will give you the discernment you need to make the best choice available. All of his wisdom is loving and patient, so don't let fear push you in any direction. Build your life upon the sure foundation of his tried-and-true character. He does not fail!

Look to the Lord for wisdom in your decisions.

Call and Answer

On the day I called you, you answered me.
You made me strong and brave.

Psalm 138:3 NCV

When we call upon the Lord, he answers us. Whatever our need is, he is more than able to meet it. No matter what the dilemma is, he is capable of directing us through it. He is the light that illuminates the path in front of us. In him there is no darkness, and he sees everything clearly.

Is your heart wavering at the steps you know you must take? Do you need a fresh dose of courage to keep going? Do you need strength to persevere? The Lord your God is with you, and he will not let you go. Be filled with confidence as you turn to him. With him by your side, you can face and conquer every fear. Trust him as he leads you and continually call out to him. When you need assurance, he will answer you. You might just find he is already closer than you knew.

Take courage in the very present Spirit of God.

Nothing Too Broken

He heals the brokenhearted
and bandages their wounds.

Psalm 147:3 NLT

Everyone experiences heartbreak at some point. There is inevitable loss as we grieve those who leave us behind. This is not something we can fix in ourselves, but the healer of every heart can mend the wounds of even the most shattered soul. Nothing is beyond his ability to restore. He can take our tragedies and plant seeds of his mercy in the ashes so that new life will grow out of them.

Does your heart need healing? May the peace of God settle over. You are not beyond repair. You are not too far gone. He gives beauty for your ashes, and he bandages your wounds. Look to him for hope, for he is full of life. He offers you the comfort, peace, and security of his presence.

Ask God to make all things new in you. Thank him for his restorative power.

Infinite Understanding

How great is our God!
There's absolutely nothing
his power cannot accomplish,
and he has infinite understanding of everything.

PSALM 147:5 TPT

Every single problem we face is within God's authority and jurisdiction. He has solutions for every trial, encouragement for our despair, and comfort for our grief. He can take the hardest heart and make it soft. He can take broken relationships and make them whole. He can take financial disasters and turn them around. His power is great, and his desire to provide for us is strong.

There isn't a single part of your life that is worth giving up on. Give God access to every part of you even when it's painful and you are afraid. There is nothing that his power cannot accomplish. Don't hide your fears or brush over your weaknesses. Give them to God and allow him to transform every part of you.

Take time at the beginning and end of your day to give God what you cannot control.

Time to Sing

Praise the Lord!
Sing to the Lord a new song.
Sing his praises in the assembly of the faithful.

Psalm 149:1 NLT

We were created to worship. If we don't give our attention to God, we will surely give it to something or someone else. He alone is worthy of our praise, and we are most fulfilled when we acknowledge his goodness. We can give our affection and adoration to many other things, but worshipping God is the only thing that has eternal value.

Worship is a powerful tool for transforming your heart. The Lord moves mightily as you sing to him and offer him your praise. When you look to him, he changes your perspective and gives you what you need. When you approach him with thanksgiving it's like opening a door to welcome him into your life. Give him your full attention today and expect that he will not turn you away.

Sing a song of worship to the Lord today.

Even There

I can never escape from your Spirit!
I can never get away from your presence!
If I ride the wings of the morning,
if I dwell by the farthest oceans,
even there your hand will guide me,
and your strength will support me.

Psalm 139:7, 9-10 NLT

We are always closer to the Lord than we can imagine. We cannot escape his Spirit, for he is everywhere. We cannot get away from his presence. His loyal love finds us wherever we are. We are never without it!

May you know the Lord is near in your heartbreak. May you know that he is with you through every disappointment and problem you face. His Spirit meets you with the abundance of his merciful kindness. His strength supports you in every situation. His hand guides you through every murky trial. What a faithful God he is!

Declare the truth of God's presence with you and look for evidence of his goodness.

No Empty Promises

"I will be with you as I was with Moses. I will not fail you or abandon you. Be strong and courageous."

JOSHUA 1:5-6 NLT

God's promises are always backed up by his faithful character. He tells us not to be afraid because he has already promised us the gift of his presence. He tells us to have courage because he has already assured us that he has everything we need. He does not over promise and under deliver. Everything he asks us to do comes with the assumption that he has already equipped us to do it.

God is with you. You can walk with confidence because he is at your side. You can put one foot steadily in front of the other because he is the one who is clearing your path. You can trust that he will fight for you because he has promised he won't fail or abandon you. Wherever there is fear or doubt in your life remind yourself that God hasn't left. He is with you, and he is the one who makes you strong.

When you are overwhelmed, remember that God is with you.

Our Liberator

"Let us praise the Lord, the God of Israel, because he has come to help his people and has given them freedom. He has given us a powerful Savior."

Luke 1:68-69 NCV

We are seen, known, and understood by our gracious Father! He has provided everything that we need for freedom in this life. He lifts us up and strengthens us no matter our circumstances. He has given us full access to his presence, love, and kingdom through Christ.

You have freedom in Christ despite whatever is holding you back, keeping you stuck, or pushing you down today. His love liberates you from bondage. Where sin, shame, and fear keep you small and enclosed, his mercy sets you in open spaces of possibility. Look to him today for all that you need. Rejoice in his love; it is your liberation.

Receive the power of God's liberating love.

Light of Breakthrough

"Because of God's tender mercy, the morning light from heaven is about to break upon us, to give light to those who sit in darkness and in the shadow of death, to guide us to the path of peace."

LUKE 1:78-79 NLT

No matter how dark the season of night we are in, there is always a path of peace that leads us into the breaking light of day. Our breakthrough is coming! May we take hope and heart in the words of Zechariah's prophecy in Luke. He was talking about Jesus. He is the Light of the world, and in his light, we find life.

In the darkness of your suffering, the light of Christ shines through. There is absolutely nothing that his love does not light up. There are no shadows in his peace. He is the liberator of your soul, and he offers you a path forward. He is your breakthrough in every circumstance, and he is always available to you.

Remember that Jesus is the path of peace to God.

Molded with Purpose

"You guided my conception and formed me in the womb. You clothed me with skin and flesh, and you knit my bones and sinews together."

Job 10:10-11 NLT

It is a deep comfort to know that the Creator of the universe intimately knows us. Not only did he put us together, but he knows what makes us tick. He sees the motivations of our hearts, senses the pull of our desires, and understands the paths we take. We are known on the deepest level imaginable, and we are loved more fully than we can comprehend.

When you are lacking in purpose, go to the one who knit you together in the first place. He knows you best. When you are confused about what path to take, look to the Lord for clarity, for he understands you better than you know yourself. May you deepen your fellowship with him, knowing that in his love, you come alive to who you were always made to be.

Spend time with the Lord and ask him for fresh understanding of how he made you.

Don't Forget

Bless the Lord, O my soul,
and all that is within me,
bless his holy name!
Bless the Lord, O my soul,
and forget not all his benefits.

Psalm 103:1-2 ESV

Gratitude results in freedom. When we are thankful for the many blessings we've been given, we won't be as disappointed by what we don't have. When we focus on what God has done, we will naturally turn toward him in thanksgiving. When our eyes are on him, we aren't as distracted by selfishness, pride, or jealousy.

Intentionally think about all that God has done for you. Make a list of the ways God has moved in your life. Think about the smallest and seemingly insignificant details of your life and the world around you. God deserves all the credit. Take notice of the many gifts you have and shower your praise upon the Lord.

Command your soul to bless the Lord no matter how you feel today.

Compassionate Father

The Lord is like a father to his children,
tender and compassionate to those who fear him.
For he knows how weak we are;
he remembers we are only dust.

Psalm 103:13-14 NLT

God is a kind and compassionate father. He is well aware of our weaknesses, and he does not exploit them. He does not take advantage of us, and he does not expect us to operate with our own limited strength. If we want to lean on his strength, we must acknowledge that it far surpasses our own.

You won't depend on the Lord if you don't have an accurate perspective of his greatness compared to your weakness. Being aware of your shortcomings allows you to humbly approach him. Knowing your weakness makes you strong as you surrender to his great power.

Embrace your weakness and offer it to God who has compassion on you.

So Close

You are near, Lord,
and all your commands are true.
Long ago I learned from your decrees
that you have established them forever.

Psalm 119:151-152 CSB

Psalm 119 outlines the beauty of a close relationship with God. If we look to him, he is always near. His commands are good, and he is true to his Word. He has everything we need, and we will not be disappointed by building a connection with him. He offers us so much goodness and grace.

It is never too late to grow in your relationship with the Lord. Whether or not you've experienced the confidence of his closeness on a regular basis, you can cultivate a deeper relationship with him now. When you surrender your life to him, the Spirit of God is within you. He is closer than the air you breathe, and he offers you uninterrupted fellowship with the Lord.

Thank God for his presence with you and press in for deeper revelation of his nearness.

Revelation Light

I rise at midnight to thank you
for your just regulations.

Psalm 119:62 NLT

God's ways are just and perfect. He alone can see the ins and outs of every situation on earth. He sees each and every heart, and he is a flawless judge. He understands details that we cannot see, and he is a master of nuances that we cannot comprehend. When we are at a loss or can't see a way forward, he is the light we need.

Don't overlook the incredible gift of God's wisdom. He longs to lead you through each of your days. Every problem you face is an opportunity to partner with him and surrender to his instructions. Every moment of grief, heartache, and confusion is a chance to experience his all-encompassing love, kindness, and peace.

Turn to the Lord when you are plagued by confusion or frustration.

Good and Beautiful

Everything you do is beautiful,
flowing from your goodness;
teach me the power of your wonderful words!

Psalm 119:68 TPT

Everything God does is beautiful. We may not always understand how he moves, and we might even think certain things should be done differently. If we want to remain faithful to him we must recognize the truth despite our initial reaction to his plans. The truth is that he is good, and everything he does stems from the perfection of his character and his unending love for us.

The is freedom in the ability to surrender your need for answers. There will surely be many things in your life that don't line up with your preferences. When you are tempted to be disappointed, remember that God's goodness doesn't always look how you expect it to. That doesn't mean it doesn't exist or that your life is exempt from his provision and care. Stand upon the truth and look for evidence of God's goodness everywhere.

Don't limit God's goodness to your expectations.

Instruction in Suffering

My suffering was good for me,
for it taught me to pay attention to your decrees.

PSALM 119:71 NLT

We often expect children to experience growth through consequences and discipline. We try to show them how to learn from their mistakes and move forward in a healthy way. Somehow as adults, we forget that suffering and consequences produce fruit in our lives as well. Just because we are older doesn't mean we are exempt from growth and change.

You will find joy, confidence, and contentment by learning how to suffer. As you embrace weakness and make room for God to move in your life, you will experience his great compassion and mercy. The more you learn to look to him in your weakness, the more you will be empowered by his grace. His glory is made even more visible when you lean on him through times of suffering.

List three things that suffering has taught you about yourself and about God.

Peace and Contentment

If the whole body were an eye, it would not be able to hear… If each part of the body were the same part, there would be no body. But truly God put all the parts, each one of them, in the body as he wanted them.

1 Corinthians 12:17-18 NCV

Each person has a purpose within the body of Christ. Each believer plays a specific and valuable part. Comparing ourselves with one another steals our joy and sense of satisfaction. We glorify God when we operate within our gifts and walk along the path he designed for each of us.

God knows you inside and out. He knows what gifts he's given you, and he knows exactly what your life should look like. Instead of striving for your own version of success, ask him for his perspective. Diligently seek him and allow him to cultivate fruit within your life. Stay in your lane and peacefully live the life he designed for you.

What gifts has God given you?

Steady Gaze

I look up to the hills,
but where does my help come from?
My help comes from the Lord,
who made heaven and earth.

Psalm 121:1-2 NCV

If we want to drive in a straight line, we can't look to the left or right. If we want to run a race well, we must keep our eyes on the finish line. If we want to reach our goals, we can't be distracted by what everyone else is doing. We all wander toward our gaze. Our relationship with the Lord is the same. If we keep our eyes on him, we will get closer to him.

If your relationship with God is your top priority, you must keep your gaze steady. Look to him for help in every situation. Acknowledge his goodness every day. Praise him because he is worthy and saturate your life with his Word. The more you train your eyes to focus on the Lord, the easier it becomes to say no to distractions and temptations. Look to him and he will strengthen you.

What has been capturing your attention lately?

Keeper of the Watch

The LORD keeps you from all harm
and watches over your life.
The LORD keeps watch over you as you come and go,
both now and forever.

PSALM 121:7-8 NLT

We cannot be alert at all times. We grow tired, and we need sleep. We need to rely on others to keep watch for us when we cannot. When we are vulnerable, we must depend on the help of those around us to keep us safe. In the same way, we rely on God to keep watch over us. He never tires, and his attention doesn't wander. He sees everything at all times. Nothing escapes his notice.

You can trust God to watch over your coming and our going. You can trust him to watch over every area of your life. You might be surprised by your circumstances, but he is never caught unaware. Though you may jump to worst case scenarios, he is always with you in the midst of your trials and troubles. When you are weak, he is still strong.

When you see someone in need, offer a helping hand.

Guarded by God

The LORD keeps you from all harm
and watches over your life.
The LORD keeps watch over you as you come and go,
both now and forever.

PSALM 121:7-8 NLT

The God of the universe watches over us. He has infinite power, yet he uses his time to keep us from harm and guide us through our days. He pays attention to the smallest details, and he faithfully shows us which way to go. He is not selfish, inattentive, or aloof. He longs to be an active participant in every area of our lives.

Let God's attention fill you with awe and wonder. Let his mindfulness cause you to feel loved and provided for. You are under his watchful care, and he will not let your foot slip. As you devote your life to him, he promises to keep you from harm. He holds you securely in his hands, and you can depend on him both now and forever.

Thank God for his protection over your life.

Wonderfully Made

You created my inmost being;
you knit me together in my mother's womb.
I praise you because I am
fearfully and wonderfully made;
your works are wonderful, I know that full well.

PSALM 139:13-14 NIV

We are God's masterpiece. He took time creating each of us. Scripture says he knit us together. He carefully put each piece into place. God created us bit by bit and stitch by stitch. He didn't take shortcuts, and he didn't make mistakes. Every person is a testimony of his goodness and glory.

When you think about yourself do you see yourself as a work of art? You are fearfully and wonderfully made. If you struggle with your sense of self-worth, God wants to heal you. He longs for you to see yourself how he sees you. Ask him to show you his perspective and he will. He is fully capable of transforming your heart even in relation to how you view yourself.

Offer God your insecurity and allow him to replace it with truth.

MAY 28

He Sees It All

You discern my going out and my lying down;
you are familiar with all my ways.
Before a word is on my tongue,
you, LORD, know it completely.
You hem me in behind and before,
and you lay your hand upon me.

PSALM 139:3-5 NIV

God is familiar with all our ways. He understands each of our quirks, and he knows why we have certain habits. He knows us fully, and he loves us completely. We are not a mystery to him. We don't have to explain ourselves or wonder if he will misunderstand us. He sees us clearly, and he watches over us with tender loving care.

You've probably experienced many miscommunications in your life. You know the frustration of being misunderstood or misinterpreted. Those things can make you feel alone or overlooked. You don't ever have to worry about that with God. He sees deep into your heart, and he is familiar with all of your ways. You are known by your Maker; you are never misunderstood.

Thank God for his consistent presence and love.

Constant Meditation

One generation will declare your works to the next
and will proclaim your mighty acts.
I will speak of your splendor and glorious majesty
and your wondrous works.

Psalm 145:4-5 CSB

Each generation tastes the goodness of God as he reveals himself to them in faithfulness. We can learn from the people who have gone before us. We can see God's faithfulness through the ages. We can be encouraged by how he intervened on behalf of his people, and we can expect him to do the same for us.

When you need encouragement, look at the lives of the people around you. Each person has a unique testimony of how God has shown up for them. Generation after generation declares his greatness and displays his glory. By honoring each person's story, you can experience more miracles than you would on your own.

Trade testimonies with someone today.

All the Earth

Tremble before Him, all the earth. The world also is firmly established, It shall not be moved. Let the heavens rejoice, and let the earth be glad; and let them say among the nations, "The LORD reigns."

1 CHRONICLES 16:30-31 NKJV

Everything under the sun is in God's control. He has established the earth, and he is the one who sustains it. As we acknowledge his sovereignty, our hearts should be filled with gratitude. We cannot possibly hold the world together like God does. We need him more than we can understand. We are dependent upon him, and he is worthy of our praise.

Rejoice before the Lord today. Take in all that he has made and give him the glory for all he does. Talk about his great works with others and give him the credit he is due. He rules supremely over all the earth, yet he loves you with great compassion and kindness. There is no one else like him.

Watch the sun set and let it fill your heart with praise.

In His Hands

The Lord is a great God,
and a great King above all gods.
In his hand are the depths of the earth;
the heights of the mountains are his also.
The sea is his, for he made it,
and his hands formed the dry land.

Psalm 95:3-5 ESV

Each season of life has hills, valleys, triumphs, and defeats. May we look at our experiences through the lens of God's mercy. He is faithful to guide us no matter what our physical circumstances are. He shows up when we need him most, and he gives us grace to move forward. He is a great God, and we can trust that if he is sovereign over all the earth, he has what it takes to guide us through life.

If God can hold the depths of the earth in his hands, he can hold your life. If he can also sustain the mountains and the seas, he can sustain you. If he can create dry land with his words, he can speak directly to your heart when you need it most. Reflect on God's greatness and let it fill you with confidence and hope.

Declare God's greatness and offer him your heartfelt worship.

June

The Lord is my strength and shield.
I trust him with all my heart.
He helps me, and my heart is filled with joy.
I burst out in songs of thanksgiving.

Psalm 28:7 NLT

Eyes Fixed

I keep my eyes always on the Lord.
With him at my right hand, I will not be shaken.
Therefore my heart is glad and my tongue rejoices;
my body also will rest secure.

Psalm 16:8-9 NIV

When we are constantly distracted by the lives of others, we fall into patterns of jealousy and discontent. The more we compare ourselves with the failures and success of the people around us, the more difficult it is to see what God is doing in our own lives. When we choose to focus on the Lord, the problems of the world begin to fade away.

If you don't deliberately seek the Lord, you will miss the multitude of ways he is moving all around you. He is constantly intervening on your behalf, but you won't notice if your happiness is wrapped up in what you do or don't have. The more you look to him, the more you will see that he is leading you perfectly.

Start and end your day by looking to Jesus.

JUNE 2

Rich Soil

He shall be like a tree planted by the waters,
Which spreads out its roots by the river,
And will not fear when heat comes;
But its leaf will be green,
And will not be anxious in the year of drought,
Nor will cease from yielding fruit.

Jeremiah 17:7-8 NKJV

God graciously gives us everything we need. When we depend on him, we are like trees planted by streams of water. We don't have to look far for nourishment, and we don't have to strive for refreshment. We don't have to muster up fruit on our own, and we don't have to worry about what the future might bring. In God's presence, we are more than adequately provided for.

When you recognize all that God does for you, there isn't as much room for anxiety, fear, worry, or comparison. When you see firsthand that God is capable of taking care of you, your perspective is transformed. Notice his extraordinary provision and turn toward him in gratitude.

How has God provided for you?

Shielded by God

God's way is perfect.
All the LORD's promises prove true.
He is a shield for all who look to him for protection.
For who is God except the LORD?
Who but our God is a solid rock?

PSALM 18:30-31 NLT

Sometimes hope feels like a commodity we just can't grab a hold of. Peace can feel elusive and out of reach. With so much trouble in the world around us and a constant barrage of bad news streaming from various sources, we can forget to look for the good news. When the world has us down, let's remember that there is more at work than meets the eye.

Scripture reminds you that God is always near. He has promised to wipe every tear from every eye when he ushers in his eternal kingdom. The hope you have to look forward to may feel out of reach, but his presence is ever so close. He is a shield for those who look to him, and he will not go back on his word.

Find safety and peace in God's presence today.

JUNE 4

Slow Down

"Come away by yourselves to a secluded place and rest a little while."

MARK 6:31 NASB

Rest is essential to our well-being. Not only do our bodies need time to recuperate from our work, but our spirits and souls need a break as well. When we prioritize rest, we create space or margin within our lives. Margins can be used for regaining strength, spending time with the Lord, and even appreciating the work we've done.

You weren't designed to embrace a continuous hustle. If you find yourself constantly working toward the next goal without even taking time to appreciate your previous victory, it might be time to evaluate your lifestyle. Everyone needs time to slow down and breathe.

Carve out an hour in your day to lay aside responsibilities and truly rest.

Many Nations

"Sing and rejoice, O daughter of Zion! For behold, I am coming and I will dwell in your midst," says the Lord. "Many nations shall be joined to the Lord in that day, and they shall become My people. And I will dwell in your midst. Then you will know that the Lord of hosts has sent Me to you."

Zechariah 2:10-11 NKJV

The Messiah's arrival was prophesied long before he walked the earth. The prophetic declaration in this passage from Zechariah foreshadows the coming of Jesus. He has made a way for every nation, tribe, family, and soul to come to the Father. He is the path to fellowship with God, and he has eliminated every obstacle that stood in the way.

All are welcome in the presence of God. All are invited into his kingdom through Christ. One day every nation will bow before him, and we will experience the glory of worshipping him together. He will be our God, and we will be his people. Be filled with hope and anticipation for that day.

Take time to dwell on the return of Jesus.

Each Season

"Arise, my love, my beautiful one,
and come away,
for behold, the winter is past;
the rain is over and gone.
The flowers appear on the earth,
the time of singing has come."

SONG OF SOLOMON 2:10-12 ESV

God has good things in store for those who follow him. There are no trials that will last forever or winter seasons that won't turn into spring. When our hope is firmly anchored in Jesus, we can trust that he is constantly leading us toward the ultimate fulfillment of God's promises.

Take heart and know that your current struggles will come to an end. If you are following God's guidance, you can be confident that he will carry you through whatever you are facing. If you ask him, he will give you what you need to persevere and fill you with hope for what's to come. He is capable of bringing you through this season in one piece and equipping you for the next one.

Thank God for the season you are in and expect him to carry you through.

By Grace Alone

The grace of God has appeared that offers salvation to all people. It teaches us to say "No" to ungodliness and worldly passions, and to live self-controlled, upright and Godly lives in this present age.

TITUS 2:11-12 NIV

Christianity doesn't have anything to do with our own skills or abilities. What we bring to the table pales in comparison to what God brings to the table. We give him our endless list of weaknesses, and he showers us with grace. We give him our sins and our failures, and he extends mercy.

While your failures might be great, God's grace is greater. He has given you everything you need to follow him. If you allow him to, he will strengthen you from the inside out. By his Spirit, he equips you to do the right thing. You aren't expected to strive for perfection. Instead remember that God's grace is the reason you can say no to sin.

In what area can you move from depending on yourself to depending on God's grace?

Always a Reason

I rejoice because you rescued me.
No one is holy like the LORD!
There is no one besides you;
there is no Rock like our God.

1 SAMUEL 2:1-2 NLT

Even on days when nothing seems to be going right, we can praise the Lord. We can honor him even when our circumstances are disappointing, or our lives don't look how we want. He is worthy of our praise because his holiness sets him above us. He is worthy of our worship because there is no one like him. He is worthy of our lives because he has rescued each of us from a pit we couldn't escape from.

When you praise God, your eyes move from your circumstances to his glory. As you focus on his goodness, the sting of frustration begins to fade. Worshipping God might not change your circumstances, but it will change your perspective and your heart. Turn toward the Lord and let your praise shift the trajectory of your day.

Sing a song of praise to the Lord.

He Cares

Pray for all people. Ask God for the things people need, and be thankful to him. You should pray for kings and for all who have authority. Pray for the leaders so that we can have quiet and peaceful lives—lives full of worship and respect for God.

1 Timothy 2:1-2 NLT

God cares about the menial things that make up our days, and he cares about how the choices of others impact our lives. He cares about what we eat, and he cares about the government. He is not uninvolved, aloof, or too busy to notice what is going. He is interested and invested in the lives of his children.

When you bring your needs and the needs of others before the Lord, you can trust that you have a captive audience. His ears are attuned to your cries, and he is not annoyed by your requests. Ask him boldly for provision and thank him for the ways he has already moved in your life. Pray for the people around you and surrender each of your problems into his hands.

Pray for the needs of others to be met and pray for our leaders in the government.

God's Dwelling

"God's dwelling place is now among the people, and he will dwell with them. 'He will wipe every tear from their eyes. There will be no more death' or mourning or crying or pain, for the old order of things has passed away."

REVELATION 21:3-4 NIV

We are all familiar with the pain of death and loss. We mourn, cry, and long for the perfection we were made for. Each of us is intimately aware that this world is far from perfect. The sting of reality is acute, and our suffering reminds us that this is not our home.

You were created to experience the perfection of God's presence. You were made to walk with him and live an abundant life. You were made to thrive with the riches of God's kingdom. When you feel as though life is nothing but pain, remember that better days are coming. You are not wrong for noticing the disparity between what you have and what you long for. Let your current suffering fill you with indignant hope as you depend on God for strength.

Thank God for his coming kingdom and for the fullness of hope that awaits you.

Oasis of Peace

The Lord is my shepherd;
I have all that I need.
He lets me rest in green meadows;
he leads me beside peaceful streams.

Psalm 23:1-2 NLT

When we find our hearts are heavy, let us turn to our Shepherd and best friend. Jesus is the Good Shepherd, always leading us in the pathways of his peace and love. Even when we pass through valleys, he guides in his kindness. In him, there is more than enough for all that we need. He is our source, and he is the wisest leader and most trusted confidant we will ever know.

Today, if you are weighed down by worry, follow the Lord to a place of rest. There, luxurious love will restore and revive you. He truly is better than you can imagine. Lay down your burdens and rest in his presence.

What does rest look like for you?

Heaven and Earth

"I am a God who is near," says the LORD.
"I am also a God who is far away.
No one can hide where I cannot see him,"
says the LORD.
"I fill all of heaven and earth," says the LORD.

JEREMIAH 23:23-24 NCV

The Lord's greatness is beyond comprehension. He fills the universe, and yet it cannot hold him. He is everywhere by his Spirit, and yet he cannot be contained by our boundaries and limitations. He is so much greater than our understanding. Even our wildest imaginings of his vast power cannot compare to the immensity of his being.

Hold every problem up against the matchless power of God. Dare to imagine that God is as good as he says he is, as thoroughly available as he promises, and as mighty as his resurrection life indicates. There is nowhere you can hide from him, for he fills all of heaven and earth. There is no need to hide, for he promises to receive you with mercy and grace.

Look to the sky when you pray today, remembering how infinite God is.

How Wonderful

I come to your altar, O Lord,
singing a song of thanksgiving
and telling of all your wonders.

Psalm 26:6-7 NLT

The wonders of God bring us to a place of worship. Gratitude fills our hearts when we consider the work of his hands and what he has done in our lives and relationships. His restorative and redemptive power makes everything new, and we catch glimpses of his goodness as his mercy meets us in the details of our lives.

How wondrous that God dwells with you through his Spirit! How glorious that you can know and worship him in spirit and in truth! Praise him for the good that he's done. Praise him for the way he works his redemption through your life. There is nothing and no one too far gone. He is your hope, strength, and source of life.

Offer God your heartfelt thanks.

Wholehearted Devotion

"You will call on me and come and pray to me,
and I will listen to you.
You will seek me and find me
when you seek me with all your heart."

JEREMIAH 29:12-13 NIV

It is not foolish to rely on God's help, and it is not irresponsible to ask for his wisdom. We can seek him even in our questioning. We can turn to him in prayer even when we are wrestling with something. He welcomes our questions. We don't have to have it all figured out or know what we believe about every theological concept. Let's simply press into knowing him more.

What holds you back from coming to God? What keeps you from praying? Do you have questions, doubts, or disappointments? Bring them along! Instead of letting them build a barrier between you and God, bring them as an offering. Hand them to him, come to him continually, and pray to him whenever you think of it.

Offer God the honesty of your hesitations.

Fleeting and Valuable

"Who am I and who are my people that we should be able to offer as generously as this? For all things come from You, and from Your hand we have given to You. For we are strangers before You, and temporary residents, as all our fathers were; our days on the earth are like a shadow."

1 Chronicles 29:14-15 NASB

Life is short. It is fleeting and fragile even when the days drag on or certain seasons seem to last forever. If we get lost in the patterns of our days without acknowledging the bigger picture, we will miss out on a multitude of treasures. There is so much value to be found in embracing the time we have simply because we don't know how much of it we will be given.

Though it might sound trite or cliché, hold each moment of your life with thanksgiving and wonder. Don't forget that God alone knows the number of your days. As you turn toward him with gratitude, it becomes easier to look at your time as a gift rather than a burden. May you find a sense of purpose and satisfaction in surrendering each moment of time to your Maker.

How can you cherish your time today?

In Your Midst

The Lord has taken away the judgments against you; he has cleared away your enemies. The King of Israel, the Lord, is in your midst; you shall never again fear evil. On that day it shall be said to Jerusalem: "Fear not, O Zion; let not your hands grow weak."

Zephaniah 3:15-16 ESV

Do we live like the Lord is in our midst? Do our thoughts and actions reflect an accurate understanding of his nearness, or do we allow ourselves to be controlled by fear, worry, insecurity, and doubt? When we truly recognize that God is with us at all times, it changes everything.

God isn't waiting for you to make a mistake. He isn't watching you with disappointment or judgment. His awareness of you is meant to be a source of comfort and strength. He is with you because he loves you. He is near because he wants to help you. He longs to be present in every moment of your day because you are his beloved child, and he is your kind and attentive Father.

How does God's nearness impact your life?

Yet I Will

Even though the fig trees have no blossoms,
and there are no grapes on the vines;
even though the olive crop fails,
and the fields lie empty and barren;
even though the flocks die in the fields,
and the cattle barns are empty,
yet I will rejoice in the LORD!

HABAKKUK 3:17-18 NLT

How do we approach God in the midst of difficult seasons? Is it with confidence that he is still good even if our circumstances and experiences don't line up in the moment? When we experience barrenness of any kind do we let our faith diminish? Our response to trials is more indicative of the state of our hearts than our response to blessings and abundance.

Rejoicing in the Lord despite your circumstances requires discipline and fortitude. Choosing to worship him when your feelings say otherwise will cause your faith to be strengthened. Finding reasons to thank him when you are overwhelmed will cultivate trust. He is good no matter what, and he is worthy of your highest praise.

Rejoice in the presence of the Lord today.

Never-ending Mercy

I have hope when I think of this:
The Lord's love never ends;
his mercies never stop.
They are new every morning.

Lamentations 3:21-23 NCV

May we find our hope in the same place that the author of Lamentations did. Let's meditate on the beautiful truth that God's love never ends. There's no lack in his love. His mercies will never end. We will never reach the end of them because they are new every morning.

God doesn't give you stale advice or make you live off of yesterday's portion. There is an abundance of mercy in his heart, and he has more than enough to feed you for the rest of your days. There is more than enough available to you right here and now to revive, refresh, console, and restore you.

Meditate on the enormity of God's mercy today.

Depend on Him

The Lord is good to those who depend on him,
to those who search for him.
So it is good to wait quietly
for salvation from the Lord.

Lamentations 3:25-26 NLT

If we depend on God, he will be good to us. If he is good to us, we can trust his plan for our lives. He is more than capable of leading each of his children in the best way. He does not pick favorites, and he does not hand out blessings unequally. He promises that he will be good to everyone who seeks him. Questioning his goodness based on what we do or don't have is simply a misunderstanding of God's character.

When you trust God for provision there is no need to compare your life to anyone else's. When you wait quietly for God to intervene, there is no reason to fret about the timeline of your life or the things you have accomplished. Take a deep breath and place your anxious thoughts into God's hands. Trust him and refuse to be preoccupied by the way his goodness manifests in anyone else's life. Your job is to depend on him and believe that he will do what he says.

How can you depend on God today?

Every Aspect

I lie down and sleep;
I wake again, because the Lord sustains me.

Psalm 3:3-4 NIV

We tend to place God into boxes of our own making. It feels comfortable and safe to relegate him to the parts of our lives that we want to. We separate our religion or spirituality from other parts of who we are in an attempt to think about God in an organized and easy to understand manner. The truth is that we are in him, and he is in us. We cannot be separated from him. As our Creator, he is intimately aware of every aspect of our lives.

The very breath in your lungs is a gift from the Lord. Your ability to open your eyes as the sunlight streams through your window is a blessing straight from his hands. The smallest details of your life are orchestrated by your kind and attentive Maker. There is nothing you can do to escape his mindful love. Let your heart overflow with thanksgiving as you realize that God himself is interwoven into who you are and what you do.

How can you expand your understanding of God today?

JUNE 21

Continual Feast

Let joy be your continual feast. Make your life a prayer. And in the midst of everything be always giving thanks, for this is God's perfect plan for you in Christ Jesus.

1 Thessalonians 5:16-18 TPT

God offers us a continual feast of joy in his presence. He is exceptionally good, and he has everything we need. The more we recognize his blessings in our lives, the more we open ourselves up to gratitude and contentment. The delight we can find in God's presence is available to us no matter what our physical circumstances look like.

The beauty of your relationship with God is that it isn't dependent on anything external. You can have constant access to his goodness as your spirit connects with his. In his presence you can find unending joy, peace, and satisfaction even when the world is falling apart. Even when nothing is going right and everything is a mess, God offers you an abundance of goodness.

Look for a feast of God's goodness as you go about your day.

Endless Supply

The fruit of the Spirit is love, joy, peace, patience, kindness, goodness, faithfulness, gentleness, self-control.

GALATIANS 5:22 ESV

As followers of Jesus, the fruit of the Spirit is available to us at all times. It's like a fully stocked buffet of our favorite foods. If we are starving, it wouldn't make sense to walk past something that would bring so much nourishment and satisfaction. Yet we often disregard the incredible blessings the Spirit provides even when we need them most.

Without a doubt, you need more fruit in your life. There is no reason to limit the peace, joy, love, and goodness that you could experience. Preoccupy yourself with the pursuit of the Spirit and you won't be disappointed. Don't pass by the gifts he longs to give you. Don't limit God's goodness when he graciously offers you more than you need.

How can you cultivate your relationship with the Spirit today?

Dance of Joy

David danced with all his might before the LORD. He had on a holy linen vest. David and all the Israelites shouted with joy and blew the trumpets as they brought the Ark of the LORD to the city.

2 SAMUEL 6:14-15 NCV

David danced with all of his might before the Lord without caring what others thought of him. He, the king of Israel, danced in the street with abandon! It doesn't get much more undignified than that. He didn't let propriety or the opinions of others keep him from expressing his joy before the Lord.

Do you let the opinions of others impact your freedom and joy? This is not to say you need to wear next to nothing and dance in the street in the name of God. Instead think about areas where you keep yourself from fully expressing your joy when you feel it. May you rejoice in the Lord, knowing that he loves your offerings even when they may seem silly to others. Shake off the shame and be free before the Lord.

Dance before the Lord.

Sacred Rest

"Let's go off by ourselves to a quiet place and rest awhile." He said this because there were so many people coming and going that Jesus and his apostles didn't even have time to eat.

Mark 6:30-31 NLT

Jesus understands what it feels like to reach our limits. He knows that we cannot operate in a healthy way if we are overwhelmed and overburdened. He is aware of our humanity, and he knows how much we need to rest. He prioritized rest with his disciples, and we can assume he does not shame us for our need to rest either.

Your actions are often an indication of the state of your heart. If you are easily irritated, impatient, critical, or consistently weary, it's probably time to rest. Let those frustrations be a red flag that you need to spend some life-giving time with your Father. Instead of feeling shame, remind yourself that rest is a holy pursuit. Instead of constantly operating at your limits, let the Lord refresh you and remind you of his goodness.

What does rest look like for you?

All We Need

Father to the fatherless, defender of widows—
this is God, whose dwelling is holy.
God places the lonely in families;
he sets the prisoners free and gives them joy.
But he makes the rebellious live in a sun-scorched land.

Psalm 68:5-6 NLT

God is aware of those who are lonely and overlooked. He does not ignore their needs, and he does not expect them to solve their own problems. He is compassionate, kind, and attentive. He pays attention when his children are hurt. Even when the world sees someone as helpless, God sees them as a valuable treasure.

You are seen and known by the God who sees everything. There isn't a single part of your life that is overlooked. He knows exactly what you need, and he is capable of meeting those needs in abundance. He knows when you are lonely, and he knows when you are helpless. He is aware of your weaknesses, and he still calls you his beloved.

Give your loneliness to God and expect him to provide for you.

Whatever We Do

"Ask all the people of the land and the priests, 'When you fasted and mourned in the fifth and seventh months for the past seventy years, was it really for me that you fasted? And when you were eating and drinking, were you not just feasting for yourselves?"

Zechariah 7:4-7 NIV

When we do something in the name of tradition or religion, let's be sure that the intentions of our hearts are actually in line with God's values. When we fast, let us fast unto the Lord. When we feast, let's do it with thanks to the Lord for the bounty we receive. When we sing, let's do it from hearts that overflow with praise. When we pray, let's look to God without caring about the opinions of others.

Don't go through the motions of religion without cultivating a relationship with your Maker. Don't become so accustomed to your habits or traditions that you forsake meaningful and dynamic interactions with the Lord. He longs to walk through your days with you more than he cares about your to do lists and good behavior.

Seek after a meaningful interaction with God today.

From the Overflow

Render true judgments, show kindness and mercy to one another, do not oppress the widow, the fatherless, the sojourner, or the poor, and let none of you devise evil against another in your heart.

ZECHARIAH 7:8-10 ESV

May we not forget how practical God's mercy is. When we show kindness to one another, we practice the law of love. When we are hospitable to the traveler and compassionate to those in need, we reflect the merciful kindness of God. Let's have hearts that seek true justice and do good to all. In so doing, our motives will remain pure before the Lord.

You are fully equipped to love people as Scripture describes because God has loved you in the same way. You can show kindness and mercy to others because God has shown incredible kindness to you. You can offer freedom and warmth to the oppressed because God has not overlooked your freedom. When you love others out of the abundance God has given you, there isn't room for hate or divisiveness.

Ask God for a revelation of everything he's done for you.

Mindful One

When I consider Your heavens,
the work of Your fingers,
the moon and the stars, which you have ordained,
what is man that You are mindful of him,
and the son of man that You visit him?

Psalm 8:3-4 NKJV

God has done wonderful and marvelous things. He has set the earth and stars in motion, and he sustains every minute corner of creation. He is more powerful and mighty than we can ever understand. His words create life, and he holds each living thing tenderly in his hands. He is sovereign over the heavens and the earth, yet he is intimately aware of each of us.

Let God's mindfulness draw you toward him in worship. There is nothing beyond God's ability, yet you are his most treasured possession. He knows every single one of your flaws, yet he finds you more beautiful than a sky full of stars. He sees you clearly, and he loves you fully.

Allow God's delight in you to fill you with gratitude.

Spend Time

The Lord defends those who suffer;
he defends them in times of trouble.
Those who know the Lord trust him,
because he will not leave those who come to him.

Psalm 9:9-10 NCV

Knowing someone allows us to have accurate expectations. When you know someone's character, you can have confidence in their behavior. If you know that they are dishonest, you won't trust them with your personal information. If you know that they are kind and gentle, you won't hesitate to be vulnerable. The same thing is true about God.

When you know God well, you will be confident of his ability to help you. If you don't trust him, spend more time getting to know him. Instead of hiding your doubt or feeling shame, allow it to spur you on to action. Do the work of spending time with God and filling your heart with the Word. Allow your faith to be strengthened by what he says and the testimony of his faithfulness in your life. Give him a chance to show up for you, and he will.

How can you strengthen your trust in God today?

Miraculous and Mundane

It is good to give thanks to the Lord,
to sing praises to the Most High.
It is good to proclaim your unfailing love in the morning,
your faithfulness in the evening.

Psalm 92:1-2 NLT

Gratitude is more than a simple act in the moment. It builds an attitude of humility before the Lord that enables us to look for his unfailing love around us. There is not a single second where we don't have access to the loving arms of the Father. When we start the day looking for his abundant compassion, we open our eyes to the possibility of his goodness all around us.

As the day winds down, you can recount the ways that you experienced God's faithfulness. How has God helped you when you needed it? How has he encouraged or strengthened you? Remember that God's intervention in your life isn't always miraculous, but it is always steady and rooted in love. You don't have to look for mountaintop experiences to praise him. It is good to thank him for the seemingly mundane ways he has sustained you.

Spend time acknowledging God's faithful presence.

July

I will thank the LORD because he is just;
I will sing praise to the name
of the LORD Most High.

PSALM 7:17 NLT

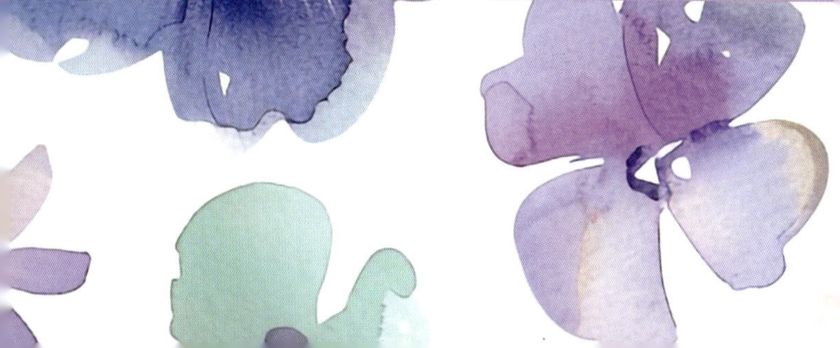

Reason to Celebrate

All praise to God, the Father of our Lord Jesus Christ. It is by his great mercy that we have been born again, because God raised Jesus Christ from the dead. Now we live with great expectation.

1 Peter 1:3 NLT

The greatest reason we will ever have to celebrate is the beautiful and generous gift of God's mercy. He is full of more love than we can imagine, renewing and refreshing us daily in waves of his great grace. He sets us free from the cycles of sin and shame that keep us from living in the liberty of his lavish love.

Today is a new day, full of reasons to celebrate! The hope that has called you from the ashes of your despair is living and active. Just as Jesus rose from the grave and ascended to his Father, so has he raised you up in new spirit life. His power has broken every chain of sin and death, and he is your victory and living hope!

Praise the Lord for how he has met you with his tangible mercy.

Compassionate Comfort

Praise be to the God and Father of our Lord Jesus Christ, the Father of compassion and the God of all comfort.

2 Corinthians 1:3 NIV

God is the Father of compassion. He doesn't look at us with frustration, disappointment, harsh judgment, or annoyance. He is kind, thoughtful, and all-knowing. He knows how each of our experiences have shaped our lives. He is not surprised by our weaknesses or dismayed by our failures. He calls us toward freedom, and he equips us to walk in his ways.

You might be your harshest critic. You might be brutal toward yourself, expecting yourself to constantly reach impossible standards. Even when you are disappointed in yourself, God is still compassionate. His gaze toward you is soft, and his eyes are kind. When you humble yourself before him, he always responds with mercy. Allow the all-encompassing love of God to change the way you think of yourself. Breathe deeply in his presence and let his compassion cover you.

Let your greatest failures and insecurities draw you closer to God the Father of compassion.

Divine Help

His divine power has granted to us all things that pertain to life and godliness, through the knowledge of him who called us to his own glory and excellence.

2 Peter 1:3 ESV

According to this verse, we have all we need in the Holy Spirit. He lives within us and empowers us to live for Jesus. When he calls us, he provides what we need. When we are running out of patience, he has it in spades. When we don't know what to do or where to turn, he has wisdom to guide us along the path of his love. Where we see only problems, he has solutions.

Instead of trying to get by on your own strength, you have the extraordinary presence of God with you to help you in all things. Don't lean on your own understanding. Instead, press into the knowledge of him who has called you. You need look no further than Jesus. He is your greatest example, and he is your present help.

When you are faced with your own limitations, turn to Jesus for help.

Commemorate Growth

We ought always to thank God for you, brothers and sisters, and rightly so, because your faith is growing more and more, and the love all of you have for one another is increasing.

2 Thessalonians 1:3 NIV

Growing up is filled with milestones. When a baby takes its first steps, the parents rejoice in their child's growth. When a child learns how to ride their bike without training wheels, they practically burst with pride! As they grow and become more independent, they breeze past many more landmarks.

In faith, you are like a growing child. May you recognize and celebrate the indicators of your development. When you choose to offer loving presence instead of harsh opinion, you show maturity. When you believe that God will faithfully follow through on his promises to you, you are increasing in the strength of your trust. Every breakthrough is worth celebrating! May you look for ways to encourage one another in faith and in love.

When you recognize growth in someone, point it out and celebrate with them!

Thankful for Others

I thank God, whom I serve with a clear conscience as my ancestors did, when I constantly remember you in my prayers night and day.

2 Timothy 1:3 CSB

In life, there are people we meet who stick with us. Though we may not see them as often as we hope, there is a bond that cannot be broken by time and distance. They are the ones we call on late nights, the ones we depend on in moments of stress and devastation. They are the ones who listen to us, support us, and who show up when it matters.

Have you ever gone through a season of life where you do not know what you would have done without the support of a trusted friend or family member? Does your heart not grow in gratitude thinking of how their presence made a difference for you? These people are a gift, and their value cannot be measured. They are a beautiful picture of God's love!

Reach out to someone you love today and let them know how thankful you are for them!

Continued Work

The Son radiates God's own glory and expresses the very character of God, and he sustains everything by the mighty power of his command. When he had cleansed us from our sins, he sat down in the place of honor at the right hand of the majestic God in heaven.

HEBREWS 1:3 NLT

Jesus is alive and well. He was with God at the beginning, and he walked the earth in obedience to him. He died, rose again, and redeemed our souls. Now he sits at the right hand of the Father and is our faithful advocate. He is still moving on our behalf.

Turn toward Jesus in gratitude. He is the reason you can approach God with confidence and boldness. He bridges the gap that is created by your sin, and he intercedes on your behalf. He is the reason you have access to God's abundant grace and mercy. Christ's work didn't end at the cross. He continues to be your mediator, advocate, and counselor.

Surrender your heart to Jesus and thank him for his faithful help.

Reliable Friends

Every time I think of you, I give thanks to my God.

PHILIPPIANS 1:3 NLT

What does it look like to be a reliable friend? Are we people who others can count on in times of need and times of celebration? In the experience of loyal relationships, we are able to catch glimpses of God's faithful love toward us. When we live with love as our banner, extending mercy to others whenever we have the opportunity, we reflect the heart of our good Father.

Are there people in your life that you can count on no matter what? They are treasured gifts from God. It is a blessing to have friends who fight for you when you have no strength of your own, support you in your endeavors, and show up when you need them. May you be someone who is also reliable in love and intentional with your relationships.

Thank God for your trusted friends!

Great Expectation

It is by his great mercy that we have been born again.... Now we live with great expectation, and we have a priceless inheritance—an inheritance that is kept in heaven for you, pure and undefiled, beyond the reach of change and decay.

1 Peter 1:3-4 NLT

We have been ushered into the freedom of God's kingdom by the great mercy of Jesus. We have been born again into the family of God. Our great expectation and wonderful hope are not in what we can achieve or acquire on this earth. Instead, we look toward our glorious inheritance of eternal life.

Look ahead to the coming of Christ's kingdom and set your eyes on things above. This does not mean that you must escape the realities of your life, for God is with you through each of your days. He transforms your heart by his Spirit, and he encourages you in the midst of every crisis. As you turn your attention to God's unfailing love and faithful nature, may your heart find hope in the promise of his unsurpassable goodness.

Remember that today's troubles are fleeting.
Turn your attention to God's faithful promises.

Precious Promises

He has granted to us his precious and very great promises, so that through them you may become partakers of the divine nature, having escaped from the corruption that is in the world because of sinful desire.

2 PETER 1:4 ESV

God has given us an escape from the corruption of the world. We are not bound to our sinful desires, and we don't need to let them control our lives. Through Christ we have freedom and the ability to live in a way that honors God. We are not limited to the cries or our flesh, and we are not slaves to our whims.

Deliberately give Jesus authority in your life. Don't give in to the lie that you cannot change the way you think or act. God's precious and very great promises are your redemption. Freedom is found in acknowledging the power of Christ's love in your life. He can take every broken part of your heart and make it new.

Don't limit the power of God's promises today.

Gracious Generosity

I thank God because in Christ you have been made rich in every way, in all your speaking and in all your knowledge.

1 Corinthians 1:5 NCV

We are rich in Christ. He has blessed us immensely. He has filled our lives with good gifts, and he promises to sustain us until he comes back again. He is with us through every trial, and he gives us everything we need to persevere until the end. We are not lacking anything because of his generous grace.

If your thoughts constantly stray toward what you don't have, you'll find it difficult to be content. If you are worried about how your life compares to those around you, you'll struggle to cultivate gratitude. Instead of dwelling on what you think you lack, focus on what Jesus has already done for you. Set your mind on his gracious generosity, and you'll begin to see the multitude of good gifts he's given you.

Deliberately focus on the good things in your life today.

Only Light

This is the message we have heard from him and declare to you: God is light; in him there is no darkness at all.

1 John 1:5 NIV

We cannot escape suffering in this life, and we can't outrun loss. We all find ourselves in the throes of grief at some point. It's important to remember that loss is not a punishment. Jesus experienced it himself. There is solace in his presence, for he knows what we are going through. He knows the ache of sorrow, and he is with us in it.

Though mourning may last for a season, there is the promise of a new day ahead. In the light of his radiance, you will see what you could not in the darkness of your grief. You will see the seeds that were sown in sorrow springing up into gardens of beautiful new life. God is light, and in him there is no darkness. He sees everything clearly, and he knows how to lead you toward new life.

Trust that God sees what you cannot and ask him for his perspective today.

Given a Family

God decided in advance to adopt us into his own family by bringing us to himself through Jesus Christ. This is what he wanted to do, and it gave him great pleasure.

EPHESIANS 1:5 NLT

No matter how loving your family is, there are bound to be areas of frustration or needs that have gone unmet. On the other hand, no matter how dysfunctional your family system may have been, there is a place where you belong. Through Jesus, you have been brought into God's family. You are his beloved child, and he loves you perfectly and completely.

There's no need to prove your worth to your good Father. He sees you as you are, and he loves you. He sees you through the lens of Jesus, and his gaze is full of love and mercy. You don't have to dress yourself up, and you don't have to earn your place. He knows you, and he draws you to his heart with gentle kindness. His love is fierce, breaking down lies and walls of shame. Come find your place at his table today.

Come to the Father with an open heart to receive from his abundant love.

Simply Ask

If you need wisdom, ask our generous God, and he will give it to you. He will not rebuke you for asking.

James 1:5 NLT

Our own pride is often the biggest barrier to growth. We stay stuck because we don't ask for help. We easily forget that God offers us unlimited wisdom. He is our ever-present help whenever we call upon him. There is never a time when he expects us to figure out things on our own. There is never a situation in which he expects us to prove ourselves or lean on our own abilities.

True strength is found in dependence on the Lord. The quicker you run to him for help, the less time you need to spend in uncertainty. There is no need to see how far you can go alone. Run to him at the first sign of trouble. He says that he will give you wisdom with great generosity, and you can depend on him to keep his word.

Don't overlook the gift of God's wisdom.

Deeply Understood

"Before I formed you in the womb I knew you,
before you were born I set you apart."

JEREMIAH 1:5 NIV

When you feel misunderstood by others, rest in the assurance that you are completely known by God. He does not mistake your intentions, and he knows every part of your heart. He created you with purpose, and he knit you together with love. He knows all of your quirks and talents. He delights in what makes you who you are, and he rejoices over you with singing.

When you try your best but fail to meet the expectations of others, there is no reason to hide in shame. Let it be an opportunity for humility and love to grow. You are not perfect, and you cannot please everyone. You can extend kindness and mercy toward others while filling up on the source of life itself. Let your identity be rooted in who God says you are rather than the opinion of others.

Let God speak his truth over your identity.

Confident in Christ

I am confident of this very thing, that He who began a good work among you will complete it by the day of Christ Jesus.

Philippians 1:6 NASB

If we are living and breathing, God is still working in our lives. He is constantly intervening on our behalf, and he hasn't given up on anyone. None of us have reached our limits, and none of us are done learning and growing. There is always more room for God to move.

Focus on this Scripture today and let it encourage you. There is so much hope to be found in God's continued work in your life. You aren't finished, and you haven't learned everything there is to know. Each day is a new opportunity to remain open to God's work in your life and to depend on him to guide you along the path he's set out for you.

Give God the areas of your life you've given up on.

Pure Light of Unity

If we keep living in the pure light that surrounds him, we share unbroken fellowship with one another, and the blood of Jesus, his Son, continually cleanses us from all sin.

1 John 1:7 TPT

When we live in the freedom of Christ's love, gratitude is sown like seeds into the soil of our lives. If we have been forgiven much, how much more will we forgive others? When we look through the perspective of Jesus, who makes all things new, our faith is strengthened in the endless possibilities of his restorative power.

Instead of going mindlessly through your day, may you be aware of the tangible grace of God. He shines on you with his glorious presence. In the light of his nearness, you can see others more clearly. May you reach out in love to those who bear his image. Don't get caught up in the divisive issues that drive us further from each other. Instead, choose to be united in purpose through his love.

When you feel criticism rising within you, ask God for his perspective.

Lighthearted Joy

Your hearts can soar with joyful gratitude when you think of how God made you worthy to receive the glorious inheritance freely given to us by living in the light.

Colossians 1:12 TPT

Our inheritance has been freely given. As children of God, we have access to a storehouse of goodness. We are heirs to his kingdom simply because he has chosen us and called us his own. We live in the light of his love, and he promises to care for us for all our days and beyond.

Let your heart be filled with gratitude when you think of all God has done for you. It doesn't matter what your earthly life looks like; you are accepted, cherished, and provided for by the God of the entire universe. He says that you are good enough to receive his greatest blessings. You qualify for his glorious inheritance because you are his beloved child. God calls you worthy despite your flaws or current circumstances.

Thank God for the promise of his inheritance.

Tools for Living

God has not given us a spirit of fear, but one of power, love, and sound judgment.

2 Timothy 1:7 CSB

God does not deal with us in shame or fear. He guides us gently with his firm hand holding ours. He does not motivate us with threats. We don't need to look for help any further than his Spirit. We do not need to go to the ends of the earth to find him. He is with us now in power and in presence.

The Holy Spirit gives you strength for your weakness, strategies for your problems, wisdom for your questions, and kind correction when you need it. He moves with compassion and mercy, and he delivers you from your fears. He is peace personified who offers you comfort and joy for your sorrows. He moves with the same resurrection power that raised Christ from the grave. He is your constant help and your forever advocate.

Lean on the Spirit in all you do today.

Abundantly Kind

He is so rich in kindness and grace that he purchased our freedom with the blood of his Son and forgave our sins.

Ephesians 1:7 NLT

God is rich in kindness. He is not hateful, harsh, or power hungry. He is not a dictator, a mean-spirited judge, or an impatient teacher. He is faithful, kind, and full of grace. Our perspective of God's character changes everything. It impacts how we move throughout our day, how we view ourselves, and how we treat others.

God's great kindness has led to your freedom. He has graciously forgiven you through Christ, and he looks at you with love and mercy. Breathe deep in the presence of his love and let it soften your heart. Experience his love for you and allow it to filter through every part of your life.

Be intentional in kindness toward others today.

Help in All Things

The LORD is good,
a refuge in times of trouble.
He cares for those who trust in him.

NAHUM 1:7 NIV

God is our refuge in times of trouble. Life is inevitably filled with storms of many kinds, but God promises to be our shelter. He shields us from the elements, and he blesses us with his presence. He comforts us when we are afraid, and he offers us wisdom when we don't know what to do. His companionship keeps us from feeling alone, and his grace equips us to endure.

Don't live in fear of storms. Christ within you is stronger than anything you might come up against. He is your anchor, and his love keeps you from being swept away. He is your strong tower, and he offers you the safe covering of his presence. Every storm is simply another opportunity to experience his loving kindness in a greater way. Run to him for peace, and he will not turn you away.

When you are worried or overwhelmed, find refuge in the presence of God.

Inexpressible Glory

Though you have not seen Him, you love Him, and though you do not see Him now, but believe in Him, you greatly rejoice with joy inexpressible and full of glory.

1 Peter 1:8 NASB

We do not have to wait for everything to be made clear in order to experience the deep joy of God's promises. We love him even though we have not seen him yet. We trust him to fulfill his Word even though we haven't experienced the fullness of his goodness. He has revealed his glorious nature all around us! He is the way, the truth, and the life.

May you rejoice in your great God and King. Remember his faithfulness through the ages and be encouraged at his unchanging character. He is the same God who delivered the Israelites from their captivity. He is the one who heals, restores, and revives. He is the source of life, and he is inexpressibly good.

Thank God for the glimpses you have seen of his glory.

Firm Foundation

"I am the Alpha and the Omega," says the LORD God, "who is, and who was, and who is to come, the Almighty."

REVELATION 1:8 NIV

God is so much greater than any circumstance we face in this life. He is bigger than our small lives can contain. His reach is larger than the farthest universe, yet he knows us intimately. He is beyond our understanding, yet he is so very near. The earth is a footstool to him. No mind can comprehend how vast he is, and no one can fathom his power.

This is the God who calls you by name. This is your firm foundation and your eternal source of hope. You are not a pawn in a game that he is playing. You are the object of his affection, and he will faithfully fulfill each promise he makes to you. He does not shift or change his loyal love. Look to him and throw your hope into the ocean of his love.

Put your problems into perspective by reflecting on God's greatness.

Faithful to Forgive

If we confess our sins, He is faithful and just to forgive us our sins and to cleanse us from all unrighteousness.

1 John 1:9 ESV

We can cling to the truth found in Scripture. We can bet our lives on God's promises and declare his Word over our circumstances. We can't always predict how we'll act in any given circumstance, but we are guaranteed that God will forgive us when we turn to him. We will surely make many mistakes, but God's graciousness never changes. If we humbly confess, he will always make us new.

There is so much freedom to be found in God's faithful forgiveness. This doesn't mean you should brazenly do whatever you want, but you don't need to live in fear of making mistakes. God knows your weaknesses. He knows that you will mess up and make the wrong choices. Instead of condemning you, he has given you a fool proof contingency plan for sin.

Confess your sin, let go of your shame, and walk in the freedom of God's forgiveness.

Holy Hope

He delivered us from such a deadly peril, and he will deliver us. On him we have set our hope that he will deliver us again.

2 Corinthians 1:10 ESV

Jesus is our great deliverer. What he has done already, he will do again. Let us look with hope to the future, knowing that the one who was revealed as rescuer and Savior will be our advocate and help. He does not grow tired of helping us when we need him. He does not turn us away when we come to him for assistance.

Run to Jesus in your hour of great need. He is your deliverer and ever-present help. Look to him for whatever you need in times of stress or confusion. He cares deeply about the things that upset you and cause you pain. You can confidently come before him, knowing he will welcome you with open arms. He will not turn away from you, for he is faithful in love.

Let the faithful love of Christ be the foundation of your confidence.

Fully Delivered

He has delivered us from the power of darkness and conveyed us into the kingdom of the Son of His love.

Colossians 1:13 NKJV

We have been delivered and set free. God's light within us is strong enough to push back the darkness. When we feel lost or overwhelmed, we can call upon his love to save us. When we find ourselves living as slaves again, we can remind ourselves of the freedom we have in the kingdom of the Son.

Your response to God will determine how you live and move. Your beliefs will impact how you think, and your thoughts will filter down to your actions. This is why it's so important to saturate your mind with Scripture and familiarize yourself with the truth. You have been delivered, and darkness doesn't have power over you. Cling to the reality of your deliverance and let God's light have its full impact in your heart.

How has the truth of your deliverance impacted the way you live?

Overflowing with Love

The Word became human and made his home among us. He was full of unfailing love and faithfulness. And we have seen his glory, the glory of the Father's one and only Son.

John 1:14 NLT

The Jesus we know and serve is precious and one of a kind. There is no one else worthy of our affection and devotion. He stepped down from a position of power to humbly walk the earth as our brother. He made his home among us so we could experience the love of the Father. He didn't sit on his thrown and simply tell us the truth. He came down to our level and displayed God's glory for all to see.

Turn to Jesus in admiration and gratitude. He gave his life for you. He set aside his comfort, position, and status so you could know the love of God. Even now he doesn't hold his authority over your head. He continues to offer you grace and mercy. He calls you to embrace the ways of God's kingdom, and he equips you to do it.

Look to Jesus for how to live in the example of his love.

Patience

Jesus Christ might display his perfect patience as an example to those who were to believe in him for eternal life.

1 TIMOTHY 1:16 ESV

In an age of instant answers, we have lost the beauty of the tension of the in-between. With patience comes endurance. Though we can find quick answers to trivial questions, some problems aren't so readily solved. Along the journey of this life, we will either learn to wrestle with God in the tension or give up. May we be people of tenacity who choose to stay engaged with the Lord even in our questioning.

In his perfect patience, Jesus leaves room for transformation and growth. In this space, there is freedom to try and fail. There are opportunities to grow and learn. Don't become discouraged as you discover new skills and find that it takes time to become proficient in them. Instead, embrace patience and implement the values of Christ's kingdom as you transform more into his likeness.

Practice patience as you trust God to transform your life.

Remember Them

I have not stopped giving thanks for you,
remembering you in my prayers.

EPHESIANS 1:16 NIV

There are people who change us forever and point us in a direction we would not have taken on our own. There are teachers who champion us, coaches who push us beyond our limits, and friends who encourage us. There are mentors who instruct us with the wisdom of their experience and guide us with their advice.

Think back over your life. Who has impacted you? Who can you recognize as a voice of reason, truth, and encouragement? These people are a gift from God! Reflect on how they revealed the love of God to you in specific ways. Lift them up in prayer and ask God to bless them as they have blessed you. Let the gratitude of your heart overflow as you thank the Lord for the precious gifts he's given you.

Reach out to someone who has impacted your life and express gratitude toward them.

Good News

Christ didn't send me to baptize, but to preach the Good News—and not with clever speech, for fear that the cross of Christ would lose its power.

1 Corinthians 1:17 NLT

The good news of Jesus is not found in lofty language or complex thought. It is in the simple truth of the gospel. The cross of Christ is the basis of our salvation. Jesus' death and resurrection lead us to everlasting life. The power of the grave has been broken, Jesus is our eternal source of hope. It is the mercy of God that ushers us into the abundance of life in his kingdom.

The good news of the gospel is life to those who are dying. It offers healing to the sick, hope for destitution, and freedom for the captive. It does not prop up powerful systems or bow down to the ways of the world. The gospel of Jesus is freedom for all who look to him. It reaches the vulnerable as well as the firmly established. No one is excluded from his love. Revel in the good news of your great Savior, for he has made a way where there was none.

Share the good news of Jesus' love with someone today.

Glorious Inheritance

I pray that the eyes of your heart may be enlightened, so that you will know what is the hope of His calling, what are the riches of the glory of His inheritance in the saints.

EPHESIANS 1:18 NASB

The hope of God's calling is that far greater things are coming than anything we have already experienced. We can cling to him through the trials of life because we know that one day he will come back and make all things right. This life is but a sliver of time compared to eternity, and we will experience the riches of his glory if we hold on until the end.

Don't quit even when the days seem long, and the years drag on. No matter what your life looks like, there are better days ahead. Through Christ you have a rich inheritance that cannot be taken away from you. Your life might not look how you expected it to, but there is a level of perfection coming that can barely be comprehended. When you are weary, look to Jesus and allow him to open the eyes of your heart and encourage you.

Look to Jesus today for hope and inspiration.

Yes and Amen

All of God's promises have been fulfilled in Christ with a resounding "Yes!" And through Christ, our "Amen" ascends to God for his glory.

2 CORINTHIANS 1:20 NLT

Every promise that God has made is complete in Jesus. He is the pure image of God's love. He is both the *yes* and *amen* of all God's vows. What he has begun, he will continue to do until it is finished. There is not a single promise that does not find its fulfillment in Christ.

When you join your heart in agreement with God's spoken Word, you add an *amen* to the chorus of those who have gone before you. There is power in partnering with the promises of God. When you stand on the foundation of others' faith, you will find our own bolstered. You will find your heart stirred with hope as you recall the faithfulness of God through the ages. He is the same today, and he won't ever change.

Pray God's promises today and let your amen resound!

August

Thank God for this gift
too wonderful for words!

2 Corinthians 9:15 NLT

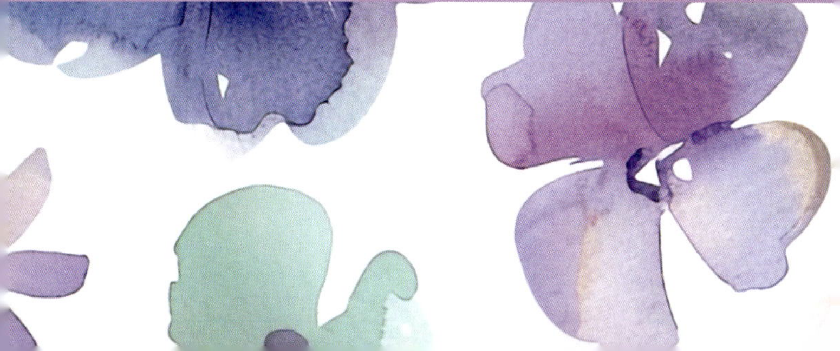

Firm Faith

Through him you believe in God, who raised him from the dead and gave him glory, so that your faith and hope are in God.

1 Peter 1:21 CSB

Our faith is not dependent on what we do. It is not based on our abilities or skills. All of our hopes are firmly established in God. They are dependent on his faithfulness, and we know that he is loyal and true. No matter how much we have failed, God is unchanging in faithfulness. What a reason to celebrate today!

May you take a deep breath of relief as you focus on his greatness and faithfulness. Let go of what you cannot control. Trust that the Lord will continue to work all things together for his glory and for your good. He is a firm foundation to stand upon, and he is a safe place to rest.

Remember that God is more than able to do what you need him to do.

Remain in Love

Keep yourselves in the love of God, waiting for the mercy of our Lord Jesus Christ that leads to eternal life.

Jude 1:21 ESV

The encouragement to keep ourselves in the love of God indicates that it is our responsibility to engage with the Lord. We can acknowledge the miraculous things he's done for us, but we must also respond. Our relationship with him is about more than simply being aware of the truth. We must turn our hearts toward him every day, constantly looking to him for guidance, mercy, and grace.

If you have felt lost or disappointed with your relationship with God, it might be time to assess your heart. Are you surrendered to him? Are you devoting your time and energy to following his will for your life? Are you giving him more than lip service? Ask God for grace to engage with his Spirit and keep yourself in the love of God. Make the deliberate choice to lay your life down and trust that God will lead you along the right path.

Keep love at the forefront of your mind as you go about your day.

Great Joy

All glory to God, who is able to keep you from falling away and will bring you with great joy into his glorious presence without a single fault.

Jude 1:24 NLT

We all have barriers to joy. There are things in our lives that are difficult to get past. We assume that if they were different, or if we were different, joy would come easily. We must remember that joy is not a result of our good or bad circumstances. God is the one who cultivates joy in our lives. He brings us into his glorious presence, and he blesses us with unlimited forgiveness and grace.

Deliberately walk away from the belief that joy is dependent on what you do or don't have. Refrain from putting contingencies on your peace, happiness, and contentment. Instead, remember that true joy doesn't depend on anything you can or can't do. True joy comes from the Lord. He is the author of joy, and the joy found in his presence cannot be manufactured any other way.

Where and how have you sought man-made joy in the past?

God Is Better

The foolishness of God is wiser than human wisdom, and the weakness of God is stronger than human strength.

1 Corinthians 1:25 NIV

Though we face our limits on a daily basis, may we never forget that God's strength is limitless. His wisdom is superior to any knowledge that we can gain in this world. We catch glimpses of beauty, and we know moments of awe and wonder. Still, the greatness of God is far greater than anything we have yet seen or could ever imagine.

Instead of relying on what you have today, press into the presence of God for more of him. He has solutions for your problems, power to help you endure your present troubles, grace to give you space to grow, and more than enough rest for your weary soul. Everything you long for is found in him. He is the fulfillment of every need and desire.

Remember God's goodness when you are disappointed by others.

Forgiveness Abounds

The next day John saw Jesus coming toward him and said, "Look! The Lamb of God who takes away the sin of the world!"

JOHN 1:29 NLT

There is nothing in this world that is too big for Jesus to handle. No war, trauma, or trial is beyond his power. His sacrifice covers it all, and those who come to him are met with compassion and grace. His mercy draws us in, and he purifies us in the overwhelming power of his love.

Is there something that you have been withholding from God? Is there an area of life that has been your secret struggle? Let his light shine on you as you bring him the good, the bad, and the ugly. He is full of power to lift you up from the pit that has trapped you. He is not surprised or offended by anything you present him with. Let him in and let him help you. He loves you more than you can imagine.

Be honest with God today about your struggles and embrace his forgiveness.

No One Like Him

"There is no one holy like the LORD,
Indeed, there is no one besides You,
Nor is there any rock like our God."

1 SAMUEL 2:2 NASB

There is no one like the Lord. There is no earthly satisfaction or personal gain that can compare to knowing him. There is no worldly treasure or accomplishment that can fulfill our hearts like being in his presence. He alone is our source of life, and he alone is the firm foundation we stand upon.

The dissatisfaction you feel with your life may be a direct result of searching for satisfaction outside of God. There is no one like him. There is no earthly relationship that will fulfill you like your relationship with the Lord. You will come up short when you search for identity in any other place than his presence. Give him your heavy burdens and allow his love to define who you are.

Run to God's presence when you are dissatisfied with your life or other people.

True Motives

We speak as messengers approved by God to be entrusted with the Good News. Our purpose is to please God, not people. He alone examines the motives of our hearts.

1 Thessalonians 2:4 NLT

God alone can see the motives of our hearts. This revelation brings both personal freedom and grace for our relationships. We can be confident knowing that even when we are misunderstood by others, God knows the true state of our hearts. At the same time, we can be even more gracious toward others because we can admit that we ourselves can't possibly know what is going on inside the heart of someone else.

As you experience God's graciousness, you will be able to extend more grace to others. The more you find freedom in his mercy, the more you will be able to look at people with gentleness and understanding. God sees your heart clearly, yet he treats you with kindness. He knows your greatest weaknesses, yet they don't stand in the way of his love for you.

How can you treat others with the same mercy God extends to you?

Covered by Love

He has brought me to his banquet hall,
And his banner over me is love.

Song of Solomon 2:4 NASB

God's banner over us is love. Just like a banner declares the title or purpose of an event, so God's love defines and establishes who we are. We find our identity, purpose, and satisfaction in the fullness of his love. We don't need to wonder who we are, why we were made, or where we are going. His love over us is steady, strong, and eternal.

As one who has surrendered to the Lord, you are covered by his love. You are not separate from him, and you cannot be taken out of his hands. There is no need to search the world for who you are or what your purpose is. You are a beloved child of God who is held securely by the loving hands of your Father.

Confidently approach God in prayer today, knowing that love ushers you in.

Trust and Obey

If anyone obeys his word, love for God is truly made complete in them. This is how we know we are in him.

1 John 2:5 NIV

When we follow the Lord, we must do more than acknowledge the truth. God is worth far more than our lip service. He is worthy of our full devotion. His Word is meant to be heard and applied to our lives. This isn't because he longs for us to be obedient. His command for us to obey his Word is rooted in love and wisdom. He knows what is best for us, and he equips us to do it.

Following God's Word is not a chore or an obligation. His instructions for you are full of mercy and grace. The more you lean on him for strength and step forward in faith, the more you will see that he can be trusted. As you follow him, he will give you a greater revelation of his love, and you will experience the blessings that come with obedience.

How have you seen the goodness of God's instructions in your own life?

Holy Habitation

You are living stones that God is building into his spiritual temple. What's more, you are his holy priests. Through the mediation of Jesus Christ, you offer spiritual sacrifices that please God.

1 Peter 2:5 NLT

We do not have to make a long trek or embark on a voyage to find God. He meets us where we are. What a wonderfully mysterious and indescribably good God he is! He makes his home with us. Jesus promised that when he left earth, the Father would send the Holy Spirit to be with us at all times.

The Holy Spirit is your advocate, helper, and constant companion. The Holy Spirit is your strength, song, and source of life. The Holy Spirit is God himself, and he is with you always. You can't see him, but you can sense how he moves. May you know the powerful and tangible presence of God through the presence of the Spirit in your life.

Thank God for his Holy Spirit who lives in you.

Endless Wisdom

The LORD grants wisdom!
From his mouth come knowledge and understanding.

PROVERBS 2:6 NLT

Though admitting our own limits may look like weakness and foolishness to the world, it is the beginning of wisdom. When we are able to honestly acknowledge that we don't have all the answers, we open ourselves to the wisdom that can expand our understanding. God is full of clarity, light, and life even when we don't see the full picture.

The Lord grants wisdom to all who seek it. He is not stingy with his revelations. When you ask him for guidance, he will give it. A humble heart is teachable. There is no need to impress God or convince him you are worthy. He isn't fooled by your platitudes or presentations. He sees your heart, and he knows your frailty. You can confidently yield to his leadership, for he will guide you in perfect wisdom and love.

Humble your heart before the Lord today and ask for his perspective.

Deep Roots

Let your roots grow down into him, and let your lives be built on him. Then your faith will grow strong in the truth you were taught, and you will overflow with thankfulness.

COLOSSIANS 2:7 NLT

When we are rooted in Christ, we are strong and nourished. We allow his Word to encourage us, and we embrace his teachings. As a result, we grow in wisdom and understanding. Our constant connection with him is what allows us to withstand daily trials and unexpected suffering. He is our firm foundation no matter what comes our way.

As you abide in Christ, allowing your roots to grow deeper and deeper, your attitude will begin to reflect his heart. As your foundation in Christ becomes stronger, you will have the freedom to keep your eyes turned toward him with confidence. Gratitude will shift your focus from your own struggles to God's faithfulness. You'll find that the more you look to Jesus, the less catastrophic the troubles of the world will seem.

How can you grow deeper roots today?

Let Him

"He raises the poor from the dust and lifts the needy from the ash heap; he seats them with princes and has them inherit a throne of honor. For the foundations of the earth are the LORD's; on them he has set the world."

1 SAMUEL 2:8 NIV

God is not disconnected from the reality of our hardship. He is not detached from our suffering. He is the God who gets down in the dirt of our circumstances and lifts us up from the rubble of our despair. He is the one who meets us in the midst of our mess. He doesn't wait for us to figure out our problems before we come to him. He longs for us to invite him into the details of our everyday lives.

Have you been trying to elevate yourself when God longs to be the one to lift you up? Have you been gritting your teeth through your struggles when God desires to set you upon a firm foundation? He does not expect you to manage on your own. He doesn't want you to rely on your own strength. Weakness is a gift, but you won't experience the freedom of surrender if you refuse to acknowledge it.

How can you lean on God's strength?

Gift of Grace

By grace you have been saved through faith, and that not of yourselves; it is the gift of God.

EPHESIANS 2:8 NKJV

The more we recognize the monumental impact of God's grace, the less room we will have for hatred, comparison, or jealousy. When we realize that every good gift we have comes from his hands, it doesn't make sense to look at others with judgmental eyes. As we focus on how undeserving we are for all that God has done, our hearts will expand in grace and mercy toward those around us.

Judgment, hatred, and bitterness often stem from fear and insecurity. The more secure you are in God's love, the steadier you will feel. As you lean on God's grace and recognize that he alone has transformed your life, you won't be as tempted to be prideful. Humbly approach the Lord and thank him for his gift of grace in your life.

Thank God for his grace that continually strengthens and saves you.

Glorious Possibilities

"No eye has seen, no ear has heard,
and no mind has imagined
what God has prepared
for those who love him."

1 CORINTHIANS 2:9 NLT

When our minds are overly focused on what-ifs and worst-case scenarios, anxiety can overtake our thought patterns. When we learn to ground ourselves in the incomparable goodness, faithfulness, and nearness of God, we can dream with open hearts. Instead of worrying about what might happen, we can boldly declare that God has good things in store for those who follow him.

The goodness of God will be manifest in your life in a multitude of ways. His gifts won't always look how you want, but that doesn't diminish their value. He promises to walk with you for all of your days, and he promises to hold you securely for all eternity. There will be times you will experience physical blessings for following him, but you will undoubtedly experience an unlimited amount of internal and spiritual blessings.

How have you experienced God's goodness?

Called into the Light

You are a chosen people, royal priests, a holy nation, a people for God's own possession. You were chosen to tell about the wonderful acts of God, who called you out of darkness into his wonderful light.

1 Peter 2:9 NCV

This Scripture reminds us of our true identity. We have been chosen by God out of love and grace. He says we belong to him, and he reminds us that our purpose is found in his presence. We have the honor of being his special possession, and he invites us to live a life worthy of that calling.

Gratitude will flow from your heart naturally when you remember the privilege you've been given. You have been called out of darkness by God's great mercy. He gives you full permission to live with freedom in the light of his presence. Focusing on the titles he has given you rather than how you might feel about yourself allows you to walk with confidence and hope.

How does knowing your true identity impact the way you move in the world?

Simple Yet Glorious

Once you were not a people, but now you are God's people; once you had not received mercy, but now you have received mercy.

1 PETER 2:10 ESV

Our hearts should overflow with gratitude when we realize the reality of what God has done. We once lived in the shadows, but now we live in the light. We were once bound to sin and death, but now we have eternal life. We were once slaves to the law, but now we know the freedom of God's gracious love. It's easy to gloss over the glorious truth of the gospel, but gratitude is cultivated when we allow ourselves to see it with awe and wonder.

God's transformative grace allows you to live with hope and purpose. You were once separated from him, but now you have been brought close. You are not an outsider, but instead you have a secure seat at his table. You are an heir to his kingdom, and he offers you the abundant riches of his presence.

Revel in the simple yet glorious truth of the gospel.

Spirit Led

We have not received the spirit of the world, but the Spirit who comes from God, so that we may understand what has been freely given to us by God.

1 Corinthians 2:12 CSB

God's grace has reached into the darkness and transformed our lives. As we reflect all that he's done for us, we can spend less time and energy focusing on negativity. The Spirit of God has fully equipped us to live by grace rather than living enslaved by the spirit of the world. The spirit of the world says to value independence, pride, success, and earthly treasures. The Spirit of God calls us to humility, embracing weakness, serving others, and extending mercy.

When you fill your heart and mind with worldly pursuits, the fruit you experience will be dissatisfaction, greed, entitlement, and an unquenchable thirst for more. God offers you a different way. Lean into his grace and experience the joy and satisfaction of his presence. Let his light transform the darkest parts of your heart and be awakened by his love.

Lean into the Spirit's help to understand your freedom in Christ.

Signs of Spring

The flowers appear on the earth, the time of singing has come, and the voice of the turtledove is heard in our land.

SONG OF SOLOMON 2:12 ESV

Nature follows the order of the seasons, and we get to partake in the beauty of each one. The darkness and cold of winter do not last forever. It is a season of burrowing in, slowing down, and resting deeply. After a long winter, we look for signs of spring like we look for hidden treasure. New life comes out of the dormant earth, and hope is restored once again.

Whatever kind of winter you have faced, know that spring is on the horizon. The time of singing is coming again. Your hardship cannot and will not last forever. May you find yourself refreshed in the small, simple hope that blooms around you. There is beauty to find, and there is hope for what lies ahead.

Focus on small, ordinary joys today.

Faithful and True

If we are not faithful, he will still be faithful, because he must be true to who he is.

2 Timothy 2:13 NCV

God's faithfulness is not dependent upon our own. He is faithful and true because that is his very nature, and he will not go against it. His love leads him to follow through on all of his promises. They are not empty words spoken by a forgetful man. God is loyal to his vows at all times and in all circumstances.

Find hope today in God's trustworthy devotion to his holy Word. He will not change. He will not let go of you no matter how far you stray. His love reaches you no matter where you run. If you went to the highest heights, he would be there. If you burrowed into a cave in the middle of the earth, you could not escape him. He is good, reliable, and merciful. Trust him!

Dwell on God's faithfulness instead of your failures.

Ever So Near

You have been united with Christ Jesus. Once you were far away from God, but now you have been brought near to him through the blood of Christ.

EPHESIANS 2:13 NLT

It's normal to feel alone or even abandoned sometimes. Life can be overwhelming, and the world isn't always easy to navigate. When those feelings threaten to overwhelm us, it's important to remember what's true. We have been brought near to God through the blood of Christ. Nothing can separate us from his presence. We were once lost, but now we are found.

Negativity, frustration, or hatred toward others is often rooted in a personal misunderstanding of love. The more you experience the kindness and love of Christ, the more you will be able to extend it to others. The more you find security and belonging in his presence, the more you can offer the same acceptance to others. You are no longer alone, and you have what you need to treat those around you with loving kindness.

Acknowledge your nearness to God and allow it to transform how you treat others.

God's Desire

God is working in you, giving you the desire and the power to do what pleases him.

Philippians 2:13 NLT

It is God's work in us that compels and empowers us to do what pleases him. We please him when we live submitted to his love, and treat others with the same grace and mercy he gives us. His law of love is simple, and his grace is sufficient to help us.

Your weakness can either cause you to lean into the grace and strength of God or to give into the desires of your flesh. Praise God that you have access to the fellowship of the Spirit who helps you when you cannot choose goodness on your own. Even when you fail, God mercifully lifts you up and gives you strength to persevere.

Look at others with empathy today, extending the same love that God offers you.

Triumphal Procession

Thanks be to God, who always leads us as captives in Christ's triumphal procession and uses us to spread the aroma of the knowledge of him everywhere.

2 Corinthians 2:14 NIV

In ancient times a triumphal procession was a celebratory parade for a victorious military leader. The captives would have been led through the streets in order to display the conqueror's power. In Christ's triumphal procession we are evidence of victory not defeat. We are living examples of the freedom that God has secured for all of mankind.

As you surrender to Jesus, you show the world what it means to honor God and live by grace. The world assumes that submission is proof of an imbalance of power, but you are not a slave with an overbearing master. Instead, you are a beloved child, and your life is a testimony of love and mercy to everyone around you.

Share your joy in Christ with someone today.

Perfect Peace

He himself is our peace, who has made us both one and has broken down in his flesh the dividing wall of hostility.

EPHESIANS 2:14 ESV

There is no shortage of hostility in the world. There are dividing lines all around us, pushing us further from each other and shouting for us to take sides. Jesus does not join this chorus. He does not demand that we ridicule those we do not agree with. In fact, his love requires us to offer understanding and compassion rather than cold shoulders and apathy.

The love of God promotes peace and unity in Christ. He brings together all things that do not seem to naturally mesh. His kingdom is full of diversity and the beauty of different expressions of his goodness. When judgment rushes to the forefront of your thoughts, deliberately choose humility and curiosity. The way of Christ is peace, and as his follower you are called to exhibit unity in a world that prefers division.

Practice promoting peace in your relationships today.

Our Inheritance

He gave himself for us so he might pay the price to free us from all evil and to make us pure people who belong only to him—people who are always wanting to do good deeds.

Titus 2:14 NCV

Jesus paid the price for us not because we deserve it but because of his endless grace and mercy. He didn't just die to save us from our sins, but to redeem us unto him. We were created to have uninterrupted fellowship with our Maker, and Jesus made a way for us. He freed us from evil, and he calls us his own.

Reflect on Christ's divine intervention in your life and let it stir up gratitude within you. Through his sacrifice he has given you the incredible gift of salvation, and he has empowered you to live a God honoring life. He shouldered the incredible burden of your sin when you were least deserving. He redeemed you, and each day you have the opportunity to respond to his sacrifice with gratitude or indifference.

Thank God for the freedom you have in his love.

Sweet Message

He brought this Good News of peace to you Gentiles who were far away from him, and peace to the Jews who were near.

Ephesians 2:17 NLT

The gospel is for everyone. We are all welcomed equally into the kingdom of God. There isn't any division because of race, ethnicity, social status, or financial position. God's invitation for eternal security is the great equalizer. God creates unity in situations where we see differences and have frustrations. He eagerly steps into the messes we create and offers reconciliation.

Take some time to dwell on the idea of unity. Imagine what the world might look like if everyone ignored each other's differences and embraced what really matters. As you focus on the love of Christ drawing everyone toward the Lord, you might notice that you have less room to be distracted by frustrations, comparisons, or hatred. Allow the good news of peace to fill your heart and mind. Be filled with gratitude for the ability to choose love over hate.

Offer kindness and prayers for someone you struggle with.

He Knows

Since he himself has suffered when he was tempted, he is able to help those who are tempted.

HEBREWS 2:18 CSB

Jesus is eager to help us with the ordeals of life. He doesn't belittle our problems, and he doesn't shame us for not being able to figure them out on our own. He pays attention to the things that plague us, and he longs to intervene on our behalf. He wants to strengthen us in our weaknesses and give us perseverance to endure whatever comes our way.

Some of your biggest struggles might be related to interacting with others. Maybe you long to grow in loving kindness but find it difficult to treat others the way Christ has treated you. You are not alone in your frustrations. Jesus sees your heart. Instead of feeling shame for your weaknesses, invite him in and allow him to transform your heart. He loves being part of the process.

In your weakness, remember that Jesus experienced the fullness of humanity.

More Than Enough

My old self has been crucified with Christ. It is no longer I who live, but Christ lives in me. So I live in this earthly body by trusting in the Son of God, who loved me and gave himself for me.

GALATIANS 2:20 NLT

We can only go so far when we rely on our own strength. Our resources are not endless, and we will find that something has to give along the way. The good news of Christ is that he offers eternal security as well as the blessing of his presence right now. He has our future in his hands, yet he doesn't abandon us in the present.

Through his Spirit, Christ lives in you, giving you access to the endless resources of his kingdom. Your life has been made new in him, and you do not live for the satisfaction of your fleshly desires. There is purpose and freedom in his presence. Continue to trust the Lord to lead you into his goodness.

Honor Jesus by remembering him with your choices today.

True Home

Our homeland is in heaven, and we are waiting for our Savior, the Lord Jesus Christ, to come from heaven.

Philippians 3:20 NCV

It is important that we not lose sight of where our true home is. We are like wanderers in the desert of this world, waiting to enter the promised land of God's great kingdom. Though we experience glimpses of the glory that awaits us, the promise of the pure goodness of his eternal kingdom allows us to press on in hard times.

May you be aware of what you are building with your life. Are you building a kingdom with your comfort in mind, or are you building on the foundation of God's kingdom, knowing that the greatest treasures are yet to come? His purposes are worthy of your devotion. His promises will be fulfilled, and you have the privilege of partnering with him every day.

Remember the hope of heaven when discouragement sets in.

Sons and Daughters

"I will be a father to you,
And you shall be sons and daughters to Me,"
says the Lord Almighty.

2 CORINTHIANS 6:18 NASB

As children we are dependent on our caregivers to feed, protect, and clothe us. We are helpless when we come into this world, and we are helpless when we leave it. A good parent does not simply give their child the necessities; they also provide a safe space to grow, play, and flourish.

God is a good father. In fact, he is the best Father. There are no hidden motives in his heart, and his love completely covers you at all times. He is not impatient or hasty. He does not lose his temper or storm away in frustration. He always makes time for you, and you do not need to compete for his attention.

Thank God for the ways you have experienced his fatherly love.

Story to Tell

Let the redeemed of the LORD tell their story.

PSALM 107:2 NIV

Everyone has a story to tell. Every life is filled with testimonies and experiences that are woven together in a unique way. There is power in taking ownership over our history and sharing all that we've learned. We can use our individual experiences to encourage, comfort, and teach others. Even our failures and weaknesses can be used for the glory of God.

Take a few moments to think through your life. What stands out to you? What memories come up? There is power in your experiences, and there is purpose in your story. Remember how God has moved through your life and proven himself faithful to you. Honor his love by sharing your redemption story with the people around you.

Share a portion of your life's story with someone today.

September

Let us come to him with thanksgiving.
Let us sing psalms of praise to him.

Psalm 95:2 NLT

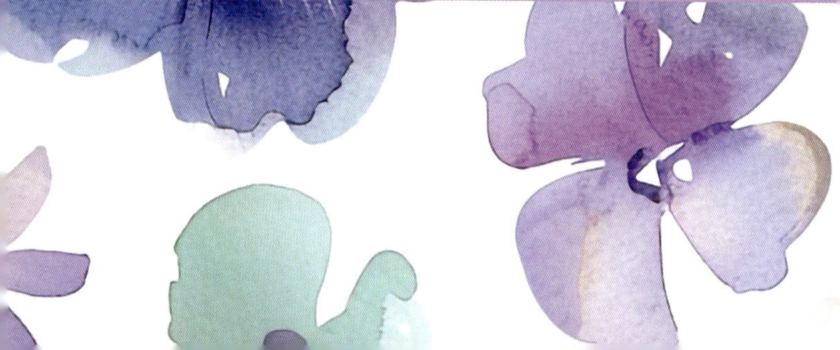

Revealer of Mysteries

"He reveals deep and secret things; He knows what is in the darkness, and light dwells with Him."

Daniel 2:22 NKJV

There is nothing in this world, or outside of it, that is a mystery to God. He sees the creatures of the deep seas which we are still discovering. He knows how many grains of sand are on every beach, and he understands the workings of every organism. He is found in the far reaches of the universe and in this very moment.

God's faithfulness is unchanged even when you worry about the unknown. He sees what is in the darkness as well as in the light. He knows every possible outcome for each and every situation. Turn to him with your anxious thoughts and yield your heart to him. He is faithful and true, and nothing surprises him. The creator of the universe is able to guide you through each of your days.

Give God your worries and rest in his faithfulness.

Refreshing Rains

Rejoice, you people of Jerusalem! Rejoice in the LORD your God! For the rain he sends demonstrates his faithfulness. Once more the autumn rains will come, as well as the rains of spring.

JOEL 2:23 NLT

After a drought, rain is a cause for celebration. After a long winter, the melting of snow and the budding of new life is reason to rejoice. There is joy and hope even in the mess of muddy puddles. The transition from one season to the next is often messy, but there is so much beauty in this passage of time.

Where you look and see puddles in your life, know that this is a sign of God's refreshing waters pooling. There is new life coming, and though it may look messy at the moment, it is the necessary awkwardness between seasons. His faithfulness comes like the rains of springtime. Surely there is good ahead, and seeds that were sown in barrenness will break through the ground with vigor.

Note where you see the rains of God's faithfulness in your life today.

Hope for Tomorrow

The threshing floors will again be piled high with grain, and the presses will overflow with new wine and olive oil.

JOEL 2:24 NLT

Sometimes, in order to look ahead with hope, we must look behind to remember God's faithfulness. Maybe we've known safety and security in our home life or in relationships? Maybe we've gotten out of a terrible situation and lived to talk about it? As we look back over our history, we can see clearly how God has moved.

May hope spring up in your heart as you remember the pockets of goodness in your life. May God's proven faithfulness strengthen you take each step forward. Take courage today, knowing that the God who hung the stars in the heavens is the God who follows through on his promises. He will not fail you. There is life and hope ahead.

Remember the promises that God has spoken over you.

Trustworthy Truth

His anointing teaches you about everything, and is true, and is no lie—just as it has taught you, abide in him.

1 John 2:27 ESV

Let us turn every question and every problem over to him who lights up the darkest night. He shines brighter than the sun, and his wisdom brings clarity to our confusion. We can trust that what he says is true. His Word is reliable, and his promises are sure. When we align ourselves in his love and choose to follow him in humble submission, we will find that the truth sets us free.

Choose God's ways over your own plans today. Submit each moment to him and acknowledge that he knows best. Follow him closely and expect that he will lead you along the right path. He is fully capable of teaching you everything you need to know. Lean on him for wisdom, strength, and peace.

Mindfully choose God's ways over your own preferences today.

Greater Things

"Then, after doing all those things,
I will pour out my Spirit upon all people.
Your sons and daughters will prophesy.
Your old men will dream dreams,
and your young men will see visions."

Joel 2:28 NLT

Scripture prophesied that the Spirit of God would be poured out on all. Some would share about what was coming, others would dream dreams, and others would see visions of God's glory. All of this was intended to spread God's message of hope and redemption across the earth. God will not hold anything back when it comes to pursuing his people and sharing the truth.

God longs for each of his children to find their home in his presence. He wants all people to come to him and experience his transformative love. It is a privilege and an honor to be used by God to share the truth of the gospel. Allow the Holy Spirit to lead you in sharing God's glory. No matter how God uses you, may your life be a testimony of his goodness for all to see.

Ask the Holy Spirit to broaden your understanding of his power.

Stand Out

See what kind of love the Father has given to us, that we should be called children of God; and so we are. The reason why the world does not know us is that it did not know him.

1 John 3:1 ESV

There are times when our actions as Christians seem ridiculous to the world. Our actions stand out when we serve others over ourselves, pursue righteousness over personal gratification, and focus on mercy over judgment. As we devote ourselves to God, our lives should stand out among the patterns and systems of the world.

If you evaluate your life and find that you blend in with everyone around you, it might be time for a change in direction. Your life is meant to reflect Jesus not the world. You were created to mirror his way of doing things. Ask God to show you areas of your life where you've fallen into the habits or tendencies of the world.

When God shows you an area in need of transformation, soften your heart and follow his lead.

Strong Enough

The Lord is faithful; he will strengthen you and guard you from the evil one.

2 Thessalonians 3:3 NLT

In 2 Thessalonians Paul offers a powerful reminder of God's faithfulness. No matter what challenges we face in life, we can rely on God to empower and protect us. He offers us strength when we are weak. We don't have to fake it until we make it with God. There is no reason to depend on our limited abilities when God eagerly offers us the limitless abundance of his kingdom.

God isn't distant or indifferent to your struggles. He longs to help you whenever you call upon him. He is powerful enough to carry your heaviest burdens, and he is able to equip you to navigate every challenge you come across. Let God's faithfulness fill you with thanksgiving. Praise him for his reliable presence and walk confidently in his care.

Put your hope in God's faithfulness rather than your own ability.

Empowered

It is not that we are competent in ourselves to claim anything as coming from ourselves, but our adequacy is from God.

2 Corinthians 3:5 CSB

We do not have the personal strength to uphold the law of God. If we depend on our own abilities we will fail over and over. The good news of the gospel is that God has bridged the gap and compensated for every weakness we have. Through Christ's sacrifice, we are made holy and clean. Through the Spirit we are made competent and capable.

Everything you need can be found in the presence of God. When you understand the richness of what he offers you, it becomes difficult to hold grudges or let hatred fester. You are called to reflect God's love, patience, kindness, grace, and mercy. Today, respond to God's gifts with gratitude and allow that gratitude to impact your actions.

How can humility toward God's generosity impact the way you treat others?

Full Understanding

May the Lord lead your hearts into a full understanding and expression of the love of God and the patient endurance that comes from Christ.

2 Thessalonians 3:5 NLT

When we grasp the depth of God's love, it shifts our perspective on everything. His unconditional love covers our flaws as he lavishes his grace upon us. The more we allow him to lead our hearts into a full understanding of his love, the more it will impact the everyday details of our lives.

When you surrender to God's leadership, he will steadily lead you away from hatred, negativity, complaint, and comparison. He will faithfully remind you his love, and he will help you see the multitude of good gifts he has given you. When you place your heart in his hands, he will transform it in his presence.

How can you surrender your heart to God in a deeper way?

Washed and Renewed

He saved us, not on the basis of deeds which we did in righteousness, but in accordance with His mercy, by the washing of regeneration and renewing by the Holy Spirit.

TITUS 3:5 NASB

If we spend too much time looking at what others have, we may lose sight of how blessed we already are. In an age where social media presents highlight reels as reality, we must fight against the urge of competitive comparison. In Christ, we are all on the same playing field. There is no hierarchy in his kingdom.

May you resist the false narrative that your choices make you better than others who choose differently. The inheritance of God's kingdom is the same for each one of his children. May you be free to live in the renewal that he offers you through his Spirit instead of being bound to strive for unsatisfying goals.

Recognize where comparison has kept you from being yourself.

In All Things

Seek his will in all you do,
and he will show you which path to take.

Proverbs 3:6 NLT

Whether or not we take him up on his offer, God is always willing and ready to lead us in his love. He counsels us in wisdom, and he guides us in the truth of his mercy. Not every decision we make will be cut and dry, but the freedom to choose in line with his kingdom values will help us.

You can make decisions by looking for the fruit of the Holy Spirit. Where there is profound peace, God is with you. Where there is loving acceptance, he is there. Where there is patience, kindness, joy, and self-control, the Spirit is behind it. Look for the nature God in the paths you choose.

Look for God's wisdom to guide you as you make decisions today.

Joy in Fellowship

How can we thank God enough for you in return for all the joy we have in the presence of our God because of you?

1 Thessalonians 3:9 NIV

There is tremendous healing in the company of those who bring us deep joy. Loyal friendship is an incredible blessing from the Lord. It is a gift to be seen, known, and supported. Acceptance and belonging are what we long for, and when we find it in a group of people, there is reason to rejoice!

You were not created to be an island. Your life is not meant to be disconnected from the people around you. You were made for community and to experience the tapestry of grace that is visible when people work together to honor the Lord. Open your heart toward one another in love instead of pushing people away in fear. There is so much joy in fellowship with kingdom-minded people.

Call someone who brings you joy and let them know how much they mean to you.

Perfect Pace

The Lord is not slow in doing what he promised—the way some people understand slowness. But God is being patient with you. He does not want anyone to be lost, but he wants all people to change their hearts and lives.

2 Peter 3:9 NCV

God is patient with us. He sees our weaknesses clearly, and he knows every obstacle we must overcome to walk in his ways. He has the perfect perspective of our abilities and our capacity. He does not rush us, and he does not cut corners. He leads us perfectly, and he knows exactly how each of our days should be interwoven with the others.

You are not an item on God's to-do list. You are not something broken that he is desperately trying to fix in order for you to be useful. He holds your life carefully in his hands, and he knows exactly what you need. He sees the path of your life clearly, and he isn't worried about your pace. You can trust him to complete the good work he started in you the moment you turned your life over to him.

Take a deep breath and rest in God's sovereignty over your life.

In His Time

God has made everything beautiful for its own time. He has planted eternity in the human heart, but even so, people cannot see the whole scope of God's work from beginning to end.

Ecclesiastes 3:11 NLT

In Ecclesiastes Solomon reflects on the perfect timing of God's work in our lives. Everything we experience has a place in God's plan. From moments of joy to deep grief, everything we walk through can be woven into a complete picture of God's grace and mercy. We can always trust that God will fulfill his purposes for us even when things don't work out how we hope.

God does not make empty promises. You can turn toward him in thanksgiving for things that haven't even happened yet. You can stand firm and know that he will do everything he says he will. Instead of allowing your present circumstances to cultivate frustration, disappointment, or confusion within your heart, allow God's faithfulness to stir up gratitude, hope, and contentment.

Think of a time when you were hopeless, and God intervened.

Living Love

May the Lord make your love for one another and for all people grow and overflow.

1 THESSALONIANS 3:12 NLT

Paul's prayer for the Thessalonians is a reminder of the power of gratitude in transforming our hearts and relationships. When we truly grasp God's love for us, it is impossible to remain unchanged. The more we understand and receive his love, the more we are empowered to offer it to others. The more grateful we are for God's grace, the more it naturally overflows in our relationships with the people around us.

Giving God your wholehearted thanks for his love drives out bitterness and hatred. You can't hold onto unhealthy patterns while surrendering your heart to the Lord. As you look to him and experience his loving kindness, you will humbly learn to share it with others. The more you acknowledge his forgiveness and mercy in your own life, the easier it becomes to love and serve people.

When you struggle to love others, ask God for a greater understanding of his love for you.

Clothed in Compassion

Put on then, as God's chosen ones, holy and beloved, compassionate hearts, kindness, humility, meekness, and patience.

Colossians 3:12 ESV

As people of God, we are meant to reflect his character. The way we live should testify of God's goodness. When we clothe ourselves with compassion, keeping our hearts open to love, we reflect the heart of our good Father. When we move with kindness, we reveal the kindness of Jesus.

It takes humility to follow the Lord. The ability to admit when you are wrong allows you to grow and change with grace. As you turn to the Lord for guidance, he will transform your heart. As you experience his love and mercy, your character will follow. The more you choose to walk in his ways, the more it begins to feel like second nature.

Choose compassion where you would rather turn a cold shoulder today.

Confident and Free

In him and through faith in him we may approach God with freedom and confidence.

Ephesians 3:12 NIV

As believers we have been given the incredible gift of direct access to God. Through Christ, we can approach our Father with confidence and freedom. We know that we are loved, accepted, and forgiven. There is nothing standing in the way of us having uninterrupted fellowship with the Lord.

Bitterness and hatred often stem from feeling overlooked or slighted. When you don't feel like you matter, you might lash out at others in various ways. The solution to this is not to muster up feelings of love out of obligation. Instead, the more confident you are of your acceptance before the Lord, the more secure you will be in your relationships with others.

How can confidence in God's affection impact how you treat others?

Leave Room

Make allowance for each other's faults, and forgive anyone who offends you. Remember, the Lord forgave you, so you must forgive others.

COLOSSIANS 3:13 NLT

Do we leave room for other people's faults? None of us is perfect, and we will inevitably hurt each other along the way. When we keep offense from our hearts, choosing to forgive instead of holding onto bitterness, we exhibit the same kind of mercy we receive from God. Our faults have been forgiven, so let us also forgive the faults of others.

Making allowances for the weaknesses of others is rarely convenient or comfortable. It often takes a level of self-sacrifice to look past the faults of others. This is why you need the strength and guidance of the Holy Spirit. He equips you to love beyond your own abilities. He empowers you with a greater capacity than you can find on your own.

Give the benefit of the doubt to someone you have been struggling to understand.

Look Forward

I don't depend on my own strength to accomplish this; however I do have one compelling focus: I forget all of the past as I fasten my heart to the future instead.

PHILIPPIANS 3:13 TPT

Dwelling on the past with regret, shame, bitterness, or even idolatry keeps us from moving forward in Christ. We were not created to constantly look behind us. Instead, we can learn from where we've already been and continue moving on to new places. We can fix our eyes on Jesus and his plans for us. He offers us healing, renewal, and redemption.

It's not always easy to let go of your past. You might have hurts that still cause pain, or you might have regrets that plague you. In every circumstance, Jesus offers you new life. He will walk beside you as you heal, and he will not abandon you as you repent. If your heart is soft toward him, he will guide you along the path to eternal life.

Are you holding on to elements of your past instead of looking forward?

At All Times

May the Lord of peace himself give you peace at all times in every way.

2 Thessalonians 3:16 ESV

True peace comes from God not our circumstances. God offers us peace in the midst of trials and hardship. The reality is that his peace is even more potent when we are experiencing suffering. On our worst days, God's peace is rich, nourishing, and refreshing. We can rest in God's peace at all times and in every way.

Hatred thrives in hearts that lack peace. When you hold onto offenses, resentment grows, and bitterness takes root. Acknowledging God's presence, provision, and grace allows you to live in freedom and gratitude. Filling your heart with peace despite your circumstances allows you to keep your focus on the Lord rather than on feelings of hatred or frustration.

Seek God's peace and offer him your worries.

As Long as I Live

All Scripture is inspired by God and is useful to teach us what is true and to make us realize what is wrong in our lives. It corrects us when we are wrong and teaches us to do what is right.

2 Timothy 3:16 NLT

In the Word, there is a wealth of wisdom to instruct us in God's kingdom ways. His Word is clear that his ways are higher than our own. His ways are better than the ways of humankind. Where we are quick to anger, he is patient in love. Where we are prone to judgment, he extends mercy. Where we put restrictions in place to control outcomes, he frees us from the expectations of others and gives us liberty to transform.

Scripture is one of the greatest gifts you'll ever be given. There will never come a day when God's Word is not relevant for your life. Though your understanding will transform, his truth remains simple and powerful. May you look to him and find the strength you need to follow after him.

Take time to meditate on God's Word today, receiving the gift of his wisdom.

Higher Wisdom

Let the word of Christ dwell in you richly, teaching and admonishing one another in all wisdom, singing Psalms and hymns and spiritual songs, with thankfulness in your hearts to God.

Colossians 3:16 ESV

When we fill our hearts and minds with the Word of God, meditating on the love of Christ, our hearts will be strengthened by the truth. When we submit to wisdom, we can encourage one another in it. When we sing our praise to God, filling our consciousness with gratitude, we connect to the eternal goodness of his being. May we lift our hearts, songs, and lives to him!

When your heart overflows with thanksgiving, it will impact how you express yourself throughout the day. Have you ever woken up with a song running through your head? Have you ever found yourself so happy that you had to sing about it? Today, fill your heart with the Word and express your song to the Lord.

Sing your thanks to God today!

Lavish Liberty

The Lord is the Spirit, and wherever the Spirit of the Lord is, there is freedom.

2 Corinthians 3:17 NLT

Negativity, complaint, bitterness, and hatred are prisons. They bind the heart and cloud the mind, keeping us from experiencing the freedom God desires for us. It's important to remember that God longs to transform the entirety of our lives. He doesn't want us to obediently follow a list of rules while our hearts and minds are ruled by negativity. He has given us the gift of his Spirit, and when we allow the Spirit to fill our lives, we will experience freedom, gratitude, and the joy of forgiveness.

God cares about what you think and how you feel. He is capable of transforming your thought patterns and the deepest corners of your heart. He doesn't want you to clean up your life on the outside and remain trapped by an internal struggle. The freedom he desires for you is whole, perfect, and eternal.

Look past your outward habits and allow God to examine your heart and bring freedom.

Purpose

Whatever you do in word or deed, do everything in the name of the Lord Jesus, giving thanks through Him to God the Father.

Colossians 3:17 NASB

Nothing we do in this life, no matter how small it seems, is meaningless. We can know the profound purpose of God in even the most menial of tasks. We can offer everything we do to the Lord. Each moment can be a fragrant offering to him.

Allow God to renew your sense of purpose and remind you of what really matters. As you spend time in his presence, let him soften your heart and equip you for the rest of your day. His requirements are simple, yet their impact resounds into eternity. With your eyes fixed on Jesus may you know the deep joy of abiding in him as you move about your normal routine.

Thank God for the purpose you have in him.

No Condemnation

"God did not send his Son into the world to judge the world guilty, but to save the world through him."

John 3:17 NCV

Jesus didn't come to bring condemnation. He came to bridge the gap between us and God by offering salvation. He didn't come as a harsh judge, law enforcer, or meticulous critic. He came to show us God's love and the freedom that is found in his presence. When we focus too much on outward actions, appearances, and circumstances, we show that we don't grasp the true heart of Jesus.

In order to show the world the love of Christ, you must experience it yourself. In order to extend grace and mercy to others, you must accept if from God first. He longs for you to know the freedom he intends for you. He doesn't expect you to carry the heavy burden of perfection. Instead, he wants you to experience the joy of being transformed from the inside out by having a consistent relationship with him.

Let go of the judgment you have carried toward yourself and thank God for his endless mercy.

He Sings Over You

The Lord your God is in your midst,
a mighty one who will save;
he will rejoice over you with gladness;
he will quiet you by his love;
he will exult over you with loud singing.

Zephaniah 3:17 ESV

When we understand the truth of our identity, it impacts every area of our lives. When we have zero doubts of God's love and affection, we cannot help but be transformed in his presence. Confidence in his opinion of us allows us to treat others with the same high esteem he treats us with.

God sings over you. He is not distant, angry, or harsh. He is closer than you can understand, and he is delighted by you. He wants you to understand that you are loved down to your core. You matter. He does not overlook you, ignore you, or forget about you. He offers you abundant grace, unlimited mercy, and his mighty hand of protection.

How has understanding God's perspective of you changed how you see others?

Transformed

We all, with unveiled face, beholding the glory of the Lord, are being transformed into the same image from one degree of glory to another. For this comes from the Lord who is the Spirit.

2 Corinthians 3:18 ESV

The most efficient way to transform our lives is to mindfully choose where our attention goes. Those we spend time with will affect how we act. What we spend time listening to and watching will influence our thinking. Where we put our mental energy will drive the choices we make.

When we give our attention to Jesus, spending time in prayer and in his Word, we will become more like him.

As you behold the beauty of God in worship, you will be filled with the wonder of his goodness. As this wonder works its way through your life, your thoughts transform in the great expanse of his presence. May you be someone who takes autonomy over your choices, for they are powerful agents of transformation and change. As you choose to look to the Lord, you will find more freedom than you can imagine.

Be mindful of your choices today.

Even Greater Than

This is how we know that we belong to the truth and how we set our hearts at rest in his presence: If our hearts condemn us, we know that God is greater than our hearts, and he knows everything.

1 John 3:19 NIV

God's ways are so much higher than ours. His knowledge is greater than ours, and his perspective is always perfect. He knows us better than we know ourselves. If we want to trust him, there will be times when we must deliberately choose truth over our own feelings and limited understanding.

Even if you are an expert is some way, God wisdom still surpasses your own. There isn't anything you can be a master of, even your own heart, which places you above the Lord. He is enthroned above all things. Peace and freedom are found when you have an accurate understanding of who God is in comparison to yourself.

Rest in the knowledge that God's ways are higher than your own.

Small but Sure

The Sovereign Lord is my strength! He makes me as surefooted as a deer, able to tread upon the heights.

Habakkuk 3:19 NLT

Life is full of pitfalls and unexpected challenges. We can't possibly predict each trial we will face, which means that sometimes we feel unprepared and uprooted by our struggles. The truth is that God knows the terrain of every problem we must navigate. He knows exactly what our future holds, and he knows how to equip us to handle whatever comes our way.

The sovereign Lord is your strength. He is the reason you can take each step with confidence and hope. He is the reason you can face your struggles head on, knowing that he will take care of you. When you trust him, you don't need to crumble or cower at the presence of difficulty. You can walk steadily through the roughest terrain because God upholds you along the way.

Let God lead you in big and small ways today.

Weak Ones

"Behold, at that time I will deal with all your oppressors. And I will save the lame and gather the outcast, and I will change their shame into praise and renown in all the earth."

ZEPHANIAH 3:19 ESV

The Lord is mindful of us in our weakness. He sees the vulnerable, and he cares for them more than we could ever imagine doing in our own compassion. He gathers those that the world casts out. He does not deny a place in his kingdom to anyone who looks to him for help and for hope.

When you look at the life of Jesus, you will see attentive and sacrificial love on display. He touched lepers and healed their contagious disease! He advocated for women, breaking the norms of the culture. He ate with tax collectors who were hated by their peers. He is the God who goes to the margins and makes himself at home. May you reflect his love by doing the same.

Thank Jesus for the faithfulness of his love.

October

I will praise you, Lord, with all my heart;
I will tell of all the marvelous things
you have done.

Psalm 9:1 NLT

Called Out

"Look! I stand at the door and knock. If you hear my voice and open the door, I will come in, and we will share a meal together as friends."

REVELATION 3:20 NLT

Jesus is standing and knocking at the door of our hearts. When we hear his voice and open the door, he comes in and makes himself at home. It is never too late to answer the call of his beckoning. He does not grow weary, and he never tires. He is forever our advocate, our faithful friend, and the truth that sets us free.

Today, wherever this finds you, may you take the opportunity to listen for the Lord and to welcome his fellowship in your life. He is not silent. He has not left you or turned away. His companionship will bring you life and meaning. His instruction will bring you freedom and peace. Lean into him, learning the tone of his voice, as well as the nature of his person. He is so very good, and he is near.

Spend time in fellowship with the Lord today.

So Much More

With God's power working in us, God can do much, much more than anything we can ask or imagine.

EPHESIANS 3:21 NCV

We can accomplish a lot on our own when we have grit and determination, but there is far more that God can do! Let this be an invitation to trust that God can take our little and do even greater things. His resurrection power is limitless.

You will never exhaust God's strength. He will not tire of hearing from you even if you call upon his name in every moment of the day. His faithfulness never grows weary. May you become audacious in your prayers and persistent in your dependence upon the Lord. Lean into his nature and trust him to strengthen your faith.

Thank God for his power at work in your life.

Heart and Soul

Put your heart and soul into every activity you do, as though you are doing it for the Lord himself and not merely for others.

COLOSSIANS 3:23 TPT

When we offer our lives to the Lord, we are set free from the opinions and expectations of others. God's approval is what matters most. We don't need to work to impress people, and we don't need to worry about how they see us. God is our highest authority, and we find meaning and fulfillment in devoting each part of our lives to him.

Let go of the desire to please others and shift your attention toward the Lord. Offer him your life and allow his approval to be your highest standard. Remember that he gives you unlimited grace, and he fully equips you to live according to his will. He looks at you with kindness, gentleness, and love. You can confidently give him your life, knowing that he will not turn you away, and he is not disappointed in you.

Commit your daily activities to God today.

Plentiful Hope

"The LORD is my portion," says my soul,
"therefore I will hope in him."

LAMENTATIONS 3:24 ESV

The Lord is our portion. We are most satisfied when we find our identity in him alone. The world will tell us that we need success, wealth, or a particular version of beauty to be happy. Lamentations reminds us that everything we need is found in the Lord. His love fulfills the longings of our hearts, and his promises give us hope for the future.

If you search for satisfaction outside of God you will be disappointed. Eternal value can only be found through him because he is the one who will reign for all eternity. Every other earthly pursuit is fleeting. You might be able to find momentary happiness, but it won't last. God alone is the source of true satisfaction and belonging.

Put your hope in who Jesus was, is, and always will be.

Rest Well

When you lie down, you will not be afraid;
when you lie down, your sleep will be sweet.

Proverbs 3:24 NIV

God created us to rest. He knows what our bodies need, and he says he will faithfully provide for us. He is a good father who knows how to help his children thrive and grow. He faithfully transforms our hearts, yet he does not neglect our physical needs. He knows that safety, peace, and rest are important.

God wants you to rest at night. He wants you to close your eyes knowing that you are loved, and he wants you to wake up refreshed. He does not abandon you when you lay your head down, and he does not leave you alone in the darkness. He is with you at all times, and he wants to bless you with sweet rest.

When you lay in your bed tonight, thank God for his peace.

Confident Trust

The Lord is your security.
He will keep your foot from being caught in a trap.

Proverbs 3:26 NLT

God is our security. He is attentive, capable, and he does not grow weary. We don't need to look for safety any further than his presence. He knows exactly what we need, and he is faithful to provide it. When we devote our lives to him, we are promised a lifetime of being held in his arms.

Put your trust in the Lord and your confidence will grow. The more you recognize his faithful provision in your life the easier it will be to lean on him in times of trouble. You won't doubt his ability to provide for you because you'll have a steady testimony of proof. Pay attention to the big and small ways he has intervened in your life and let them push your heart toward greater devotion.

Declare the faithfulness of God over your current circumstances.

Healing Is Coming

For you who fear my name,
the sun of righteousness shall rise
with healing in its wings.

Malachi 4:2 ESV

God meets our brokenness with healing and compassion. When we offer him our lives, he offers us healing. He is as steady and dependable as the rising of the sun. He keeps his word, and we can put our trust in him. He has proven his faithfulness, and he won't let us down.

God promises to heal you if you have put your trust in him. As you turn to him, his light brings warmth to the coldest and darkest parts of your life. His light casts out fear, shame, and sorrow. He lifts your head and fills you with hope. Rejoice in his goodness, trust in his timing, and offer him your praise.

Continue to trust God for healing, knowing that he is faithful and strong.

Love that Overcomes

You, dear children, are from God and have overcome them, because the one who is in you is greater than the one who is in the world.

1 John 4:4 NIV

Every trial we face is an opportunity to strengthen our trust in God. When something comes up that we cannot handle, we can turn to the one who is greater than every trial we face. He longs for us to eagerly seek his help. He offers us strength for our weaknesses, comfort for our grief, and perseverance for each season we need to navigate.

Christ within you is greater than any problem you might come against. He is your strength, hope, and provision. He has everything you need, and he offers you grace and mercy when you need it most. He doesn't withhold his strength or gatekeep his power. He wants you to face each day with confidence, knowing that that God has overcome every obstacle.

Thank God for the power of Christ's love in your life.

Accept with Thanksgiving

Everything God made is good, and nothing should be refused if it is accepted with thanks.

1 Timothy 4:4 NCV

When the world highlights what's wrong or missing, let your heart be redirected by Scripture. It's tempting to dwell on the problems all around us, but peace is found by cultivating gratitude. Everything God has made is good. Creation, relationships, his daily provision, and ordinary moments of goodness all point to his glory. Filling our hearts with thanksgiving allows us to see the many gifts he's given us.

Don't let the circumstances of the world fill you with despair. Instead, let them fill you with hope for the fulfillment of God's promises. Focus on what God has already done, how he is moving, and all he has yet to do. He has been faithful for generations, and he won't stop now. Turn your eyes toward him when you are tempted to get lost in negativity.

Receive the gifts God offers you with thanksgiving.

Share in Joy

Rejoice in the Lord always. I will say it again: Rejoice!

PHILIPPIANS 4:4 NIV

In the presence of God there is a deep, abiding joy. Even on our hardest days, his joy is an ever-flowing undercurrent. Deliberately looking for the gifts of God's goodness in our lives will fill our hearts with gratitude. Thanksgiving and joy are natural responses when we discover that God is with us even in the midst of our pain and suffering.

No matter what you face, God is with you. His fingerprints of mercy are all over your life. When it's hard to see, lean into him and ask for his perspective. He will show you his goodness when you ask him. God has given you many reasons to rejoice!

Focus on the joys in your life and let praise to God overflow!

Inherent Worth

Because you are his sons, God sent the Spirit of his Son into our hearts, the Spirit who calls out, "Abba, Father."

GALATIANS 4:6 NIV

As children of the Most High, we find our identity in who God says we are. No matter how inadequate we have felt in life, we know that God's Word over us is more powerful than our negative opinions. He is the only one who can tell us who we really are.

Will you come into agreement with what God says about you? He does not condemn you, he is not apathetic about your life, and he does not wonder whether his power is enough to transform you. Let his love cover you and bring freedom from your own doubts and insecurities. God created you in his image, and he calls you his beloved child. You are so very loved.

Give God your insecurities and thank him for his acceptance of you.

Intentional Love

Dear friends, let us continue to love one another, for love comes from God. Anyone who loves is a child of God and knows God.

1 John 4:7 NLT

The godliest thing we can do in life is to choose to love others as God loves us. This is the kind of love that doesn't give up when things get hard. This love doesn't wait for someone else to make the first move. This love doesn't require reciprocation in order to be shown fully. The love of God is unmetered, unmeasured, and always reaching toward others.

It is not enough to love someone until they disappoint you. Love is a continual choice, a conscious action, and an overflow of the fullness of God's love within you. Jesus paved the way to the Father with continual acts of surrender and love. As you choose to extend mercy to others, you become more and more like God.

Spend time with a loved one creating a meaningful connection.

Through the Cracks

We now have this light shining in our hearts, but we ourselves are like fragile clay jars containing this great treasure. This makes it clear that our great power is from God, not from ourselves.

2 Corinthians 4:7 NLT

Even though we are fragile and weak, God has placed a priceless treasure within us. He has given us the gift of his Spirit. We are not strong because of who we are, but we are strong because he lives within us. His power is at work within us despite how ordinary and unimpressive we are.

Embrace your frailty in a world that strives for perfection. Remember that humility before the Lord is a sign of true strength. You don't need to have it all together to have value or to be used by God. He knows your weaknesses, yet you are still a vessel of his grace. Each crack and imperfection allow his glory to shine brightly.

Embrace your weaknesses and surrender them to God rather than feeling ashamed of them.

His Child

You are no longer a slave, but God's child; and since you are his child, God has made you also an heir.

GALATIANS 4:7 NIV

We are God's beloved children. We belong to him, and we receive all the rights that a child deserves. We have a glorious inheritance, and we can trust him to fulfill his promises. The blessings he gives us aren't because we've earned them or even because we deserve them. We are loved, chosen, and accepted simply because we are his.

As an heir you have unlimited access to God's presence, peace, and promises. When life feels uncertain or unsteady, you can rely on your position as God's child. Give thanks today for your unshakeable identity. No matter what happens within the span of your life, you have a good and faithful Father who is eager to guide, comfort, and love you.

How does your life demonstrate an understanding of your true identity?

Not Crushed

We are hard pressed on every side, but not crushed; perplexed, but not in despair.

2 Corinthians 4:8 NIV

Certain seasons of life feel impossibly difficult. Grief, financial hardship, loneliness, and trauma can cause us to question God's goodness. When we offer our hearts to God with gratitude it doesn't mean we ignore our struggles, but we acknowledge his faithful presence within our struggles. We can walk through our darkest days knowing that his light cannot be extinguished.

You are not alone on your darkest days. God does not forget about you or overlook you when you experience difficulty of any kind. He is the one who holds you together, strengthens you, and carries you when you cannot take another step. You are empowered by his grace and held safely within his hands.

Look for rays of hope in your day.

Excellent Thoughts

Whatever is true, whatever is honorable, whatever is just, whatever is pure, whatever is pleasing, whatever is commendable, if there is any excellence and if there is anything worthy of praise, think about these things.

PHILIPPIANS 4:8 ESV

Paul did not leave much to mystery when he laid out what godly thinking looks like. The truth of God's Word is simple and not complicated. May we be encouraged with the simplicity of Christ's kingdom values as we take our thoughts captive and turn our attention to what pleases Jesus.

You don't have to listen to everything you think. Some thoughts are suggestions that you may have overheard. Others may be quotes that people have said. Some will be downright lies. When you have a standard to hold your thoughts up against, it is easier to sift lies from truth. Use Paul's suggestions as a starting place to regulate your thoughts today.

Stop complaints in their tracks and remember the blessings you have.

Great Leaps

Do not despise these small beginnings, for the Lord rejoices to see the work begin.

Zechariah 4:10 NLT

Small beginnings are where we put consistency to work. May we recognize that our dreams will not become reality by wishful thinking. Instead, may we move with purposeful consistency toward our goals in small yet actionable steps.

God does not despise small beginnings, so neither should you. He rejoices in every movement made with faith, endurance, and vision. Don't overlook the little ways you can implement the values of God's kingdom into your life. Every small surrender matters. Every choice is an opportunity to honor the Lord.

Focus on where you are and what you can do today.

Everything Matters

Do you have the gift of speaking? Then speak as though God himself were speaking through you. Do you have the gift of helping others? Do it with all the strength and energy that God supplies. Then everything you do will bring glory to God through Jesus Christ. All glory and power to him forever and ever! Amen.

1 Peter 4:11 NLT

The talents we have are gifts from God. They are not afterthoughts from him but are given to us with purpose and intention. There is beauty in the development of our talents. We do not need to deny the draw of our passions. It glorifies God when we put time and effort into cultivating excellence.

God made you with specific talents and unique abilities. Each gift you have is an opportunity for worship. Do you love to sing? Sing with gratitude to the Lord. Do you love to help others? Do it with the strength of God's compassion moving within you. Do you love to weave stories? Tell them with an open heart that expresses the goodness of God.

Whatever you are good at, do it with joy and love for God.

Creation's Story

You are worthy, our Lord and God, to receive glory and honor and power, for you created all things, and by your will they were created and have their being.

REVELATION 4:11 NIV

There will be a day when all of creation declares the glory of God. We will all worship him together, and he will receive the full credit he is due. We will clearly see his sustaining hand over all the earth, and our hearts will be stirred in gratitude toward him. We will no longer be distracted by our earthly problems, and we will see the full depth of his love for us.

Pause and reflect on God's worthiness. Let your heart be filled with gratitude and look toward eternity with hope and anticipation. Ask God to strengthen you as wait for him to rule and reign for eternity.

Thank God for creating, sustaining, and loving you.

God Is Love

No one has ever seen God. But if we love each other, God lives in us, and his love is brought to full expression in us.

1 John 4:12 NLT

As believers we are held to the standard of love. There isn't a list of rules we must follow, but we are expected to love each other as Christ has loved us. We are empowered by God's grace to lay our lives down for those around us just like he laid his life down for us. This is how we can show the world who God is.

Your highest calling is to love others. Loving God's people is more important than your college degree, job title, or ministry position. Everything that God asks you to do must be built on a foundation of love. If the details of your days don't bear the fruit of love, it might be time to reevaluate your priorities. Ask the Lord to equip you to love others, and he will faithfully help you.

Ask God to show you any areas of your life where you haven't prioritized love.

Respectable

People who are not believers will respect the way you live, and you will not need to depend on others.

1 Thessalonians 4:12 NLT

How we live our lives matters. The fruit of our lives will reflect our priorities. Today is a good day to reflect on the values that shape our lives. If we want to be people of integrity, we must fill our minds with truth. If we want to be people who honor the Lord, we must align our lives with his standards and purposes.

Consider your core values. Look at your daily, weekly, and monthly routines. Do they line up with what you say is most important to you? It does not need to be complicated; your life does not need a complete overhaul. Simply refocus today and consider how you can take steps toward living the kind of life that matters to you.

Look for how you can honor God and others with your choices.

Unmatched Wisdom

The word of God is living and active, and sharper than any two-edged sword, even penetrating as far as the division of soul and spirit, of both joints and marrow, and able to judge the thoughts and intentions of the heart.

Hebrews 4:12 NASB

God's Word is living and powerful. If we listen, it will speak directly into our lives, revealing truth, offering encouragement, and bringing conviction. When we prioritize and value the Word, we open ourselves up to an incredible gift.

God's Word is a blessing even when it challenges you. His correction always results in freedom, and his truth always brings clarity and understanding. Time spent reading the Word and applying it to your life will never be wasted. You don't need to have lofty goals when it comes to Scripture. Every piece of truth you hide in your heart counts.

Spend time in God's Word and meditate on a chosen passage throughout the day.

Nothing Is Wasted

Rejoice inasmuch as you participate in the sufferings of Christ, so that you may be overjoyed when his glory is revealed.

1 PETER 4:13 NIV

Suffering is never easy, but today's Scripture invites us to shift our perspective. We can choose to wallow in despair or give in to complaint, or we can choose to offer our hearts to the Lord in gratitude. Everything changes when we adjust our viewpoint and see suffering as a blessing.

Suffering connects you more intimately with Jesus. Even though you might experience incredible pain, you will also experience incredible blessing. The trials you've walked through will only increase your joy when Christ's glory is fully revealed. His perfection and goodness are magnified by the hardships you experience. Every difficult day is an opportunity to depend on him for strength and fill your heart with hope for what's to come.

Turn your discouragement into gratitude by thanking God for being with you in it.

Seen and Known

Nothing in all creation is hidden from God's sight. Everything is uncovered and laid bare before the eyes of him to whom we must give account.

HEBREWS 4:13 NIV

God's ability to see everything is not meant to be intimidating. There is safety and security in his sovereignty. This is because his all-knowing wisdom is coupled with incredible grace and steadfast love. He doesn't look down on us with contempt or judgment. He sees us clearly, and he loves us fully.

You can live freely and honestly before the Lord because he knows you through and through. You don't have to hide in shame or embarrassment. There is nothing about you he doesn't know. Rejoice in the truth that God sees every part of you and still calls you his own.

Offer the Lord every part of your heart.

Springs of Refreshment

"Whoever drinks from the water that I will give him will never get thirsty again. In fact, the water I will give him will become a well of water springing up in him for eternal life."

JOHN 4:14 CSB

The truth of Jesus is satisfying. His love is complete and without a hidden agenda. It does not seek to manipulate us. It does not look to conform us into carbon copies of each other. His love sets us free to be the most liberated versions of ourselves that we can be. When we come alive in the love of Christ, we are empowered to make choices in line with his kingdom values.

Let God's love springs up within you like a continual fountain. May his Spirit within you feed you from the fresh waters of his mercy every single day. Each moment is an opportunity to drink from the living waters of Christ. Nothing else compares to the satisfaction found in Jesus. He satisfies your soul and expands your capacity to know, choose, and love him.

Meditate on the wonderful promises of Jesus.

Abundantly More

All of this is for your benefit. And as God's grace reaches more and more people, there will be great thanksgiving, and God will receive more and more glory.

2 Corinthians 4:15 NLT

God's grace is always at work. He is constantly moving in our lives and in the lives of believers everywhere. His guidance and involvement aren't just for our own personal growth. As we surrender to him, other people see his grace at work, and he is glorified even more. As we experience the goodness of his grace, our thankfulness is a testimony to others.

God is moving in you and through you. Don't hide his involvement in your life, and don't be ashamed of how he is working. As you give him the glory for saving, strengthening, and sustaining you, your life becomes a testimony of his goodness, drawing others closer to the Lord.

Look to God with gratitude and testify of his goodness.

He Gets It

This High Priest of ours understands our weaknesses, for he faced all of the same testings we do, yet he did not sin.

Hebrews 4:15 NLT

Jesus understands us. He isn't disconnected or aloof toward our struggles. He isn't too lofty to be associated with us, and he isn't unfamiliar with our pain. He walked through every temptation, sorrow, and weakness we face. He knows exactly what it's like to walk in our shoes.

You are never alone in your struggles. Jesus doesn't just acknowledge your pain, but he empathizes with you in a way no one else can. He knows exactly what you are going through, and he offers you grace when you need it most. He meets you in your weakness, and he empowers you to lean on him.

Share your temptations with Jesus and keep your heart open to his mercy.

Living Love

We know how much God loves us, and we have put our trust in his love. God is love, and all who live in love live in God, and God lives in them.

1 John 4:16 NLT

When we live in the understanding of how deeply God loves us, we cannot help but to be filled with this same love for others. As we experience his kindness, gentleness, and mercy, we can extend those things to the people in our lives. Our ability to love them doesn't come from our own strength, but it comes from the heart of God.

God doesn't ask you to muster up love on your own. He wants to pour it upon you in abundance. He wants you to have a deep understanding of how much he loves you. If you ask him to reveal his heart to you, he will. He will not withhold his love from you under any circumstance. Ask him for a revelation of his heart, and then graciously share his love with others.

Let God's love filter into every part of your life today.

A Fresh Start

Let us then with confidence draw near to the throne of grace, that we may receive mercy and find grace to help in time of need.

Hebrews 4:16 ESV

Every day is a fresh opportunity to receive God's mercy. There is no need to drag our feet in despair when the living love of God is reaching toward us. The compassion of God never recedes. It is not like a tide that comes and goes. It is like a rushing waterfall, a gushing river, or a flowing fountain. May we receive what we need in the powerful presence of God today.

All that you need is found in fellowship with the Lord. This moment is a fresh start. Don't brush past this opportunity but take hold of the moment and press into the grace God offers you right now. He is so very good, and he longs for you to experience the fullness of his goodness.

Confidently draw near to God today.

No Comparison

Our present troubles are small and won't last very long. Yet they produce for us a glory that vastly outweighs them and will last forever!

2 Corinthians 4:17 NLT

Sometimes life feels heavy and burdensome. The pain we experience can make it difficult to see past our current struggles. It's not always easy to lift our eyes beyond our immediate experiences. It's important to maintain our perspective. Even our worst days cannot compare to the incredible goodness we will experience in eternity.

You can endure even the most difficult seasons when you keep your eyes on eternity,. Having a clear picture of the end goal allows you to persevere. In fact, your current struggles can even strengthen you for what's to come. Today, thank God for his blessings in your life and for the trials he is using to shape your character and your faith.

Let your heart dream about the all-surpassing goodness of God's kingdom.

Directed by God

A man's heart plans his way,
But the LORD directs his steps.

PROVERBS 16:9 NKJV

We dream about the future and make plans for our lives. We set goals and figure out how we can reach them. It is good to think through our decisions and act accordingly, but we must remember that God is the one who directs our steps. His sovereignty and guidance are our strong foundation.

Trusting God's plans over your own gives you security, contentment, and peace. It allows you to release control and step out in faith whenever he asks you to. When you acknowledge his role in your life, you can walk with confidence knowing that ultimately he is responsible for the trajectory of your life. You can respond with gratitude and joy because you know that his ways are best.

Thank God for his leadership in your life.

November

All of this is for your benefit. And as God's grace reaches more and more people, there will be great thanksgiving, and God will receive more and more glory.

2 Corinthians 4:15 NLT

Not One Forgotten

"Are five sparrows not sold for two assaria? And yet not one of them has gone unoticed in the sight of God."

Luke 12:6 NASB

What seems meaningless to us is not meaningless to God. Though we overlook many things, God does not miss any of it. He sees every minute detail of creation, and he cares for all of it. Nothing is so insignificant that God does not pay attention to it.

May you become more aware of how God is detail oriented. As you notice him in the small things, you will be encouraged by his attentiveness. Your faith will grow as you recognize how he values even the most insignificant parts of your life. There is nothing that escapes his notice. His care for you is perfect and thorough.

Take time to notice little things today.

Better Things Ahead

We don't look at the troubles we can see now; rather, we fix our gaze on things that cannot be seen. For the things we see now will soon be gone, but the things we cannot see will last forever.

2 Corinthians 4:18 NLT

When we spend the majority of our time with our attention turned to our current troubles, it can be difficult to imagine a better tomorrow. Let us learn how to let go of the need to make sense of our trials and instead look to Jesus for his eternal wisdom. Let us fix our focus on what is true and lasting rather than our current struggles.

Though troubles will come and go, the faithfulness of God's love can never be interrupted. There are no shortages of his kindness, and he is with you through every high and low. May you focus on the everlasting goodness of God despite your current circumstances. May anticipation for the coming of his kingdom fill you with hope and joy.

Focus on the things that truly matter today.

Simple Love

We love each other because he loved us first.

1 John 4:19 NLT

Thank God that we don't have to depend on our own strength. Our ability to love others doesn't come from ourselves; it comes from the Lord. We can love because he loved us first. We can extend grace and mercy to everyone we meet because he has been so incredibly generous with us.

Loving others is not a burden you must carry alone. You aren't expected to grit your teeth or muster up kindness. Instead, Scripture reminds you that the way you treat others is meant to be an overflow of what God has already done for you. Allow his love to soften your heart and you will naturally treat others with compassion and kindness.

Remind yourself that loving others is not a burden.

All You Need

This same God who takes care of me will supply all your needs from his glorious riches, which have been given to us in Christ Jesus.

PHILIPPIANS 4:19 NLT

God promises to supply all our needs. Paul testifies that if he does it for him, he'll do it for us. We can approach him with the expectation that he is happy to provide for us. He doesn't begrudgingly open his hands to us, and he doesn't shame us for needing his help. He eagerly offers us the riches of his kingdom.

God is not a stingy father. He isn't frustrated when you have needs, and he isn't annoyed when you ask for his time. You are his beloved child, and it delights him to take care of you. He offers you full provision from his storehouse of glorious riches. Turn to him with boldness, knowing that he wants to help you.

Thank God specifically for his provision.

More Than Words

The kingdom of God is not in words, but in power.

1 Corinthians 4:20 NASB

God doesn't want us to simply know the truth. He wants us to experience it. He wants his love to impact every area of our lives. He wants us to know the freedom found in his presence, and the power found in surrender. When we limit the kingdom to conversations about right and wrong or how things should be done, we rob ourselves of the incredible gift of the power of his love.

Christianity is so much more than a set of standards to live by. Don't get hung up on a set of rules that you or others must follow. God wants you to experience his love first and foremost. Everything he does is built on a foundation of powerful, sacrificial love. Allow his love to transform your heart rather than clinging to the security of rules.

Recognize where mystery meets wonder and thank God for his power.

Renewed Perspective

Let the Spirit renew your thoughts and attitudes.

EPHESIANS 4:23 NLT

It's okay to change our minds. Our thoughts and tendencies are a culmination of our unique experiences. We all bring something different to the table, and we all have habits for different reasons. God gives us the freedom to change when we need to. We can ask the Holy Spirit to renew our thoughts and help us come into alignment with the Lord.

It's never too late to shift your thinking. When you are confronted with an incorrect way of doing something, you can choose to respond with humility or stubbornness. You can remain soft toward the Holy Spirit's conviction, or you can insist that you know best. The more you open yourself up to the wise and gentle correction of God, the more you open yourself up to the blessings of living according to his Word.

Let the Spirit challenge and renew your thoughts.

It's Time

"The time is coming—indeed it's here now—when true worshipers will worship the Father in spirit and in truth. The Father is looking for those who will worship him that way."

John 4:23 NLT

Our worship is not limited to a specific location, time, or event. It's a posture of our hearts. We were created to offer our lives to the Lord in a continuous act of worship. Jesus reminds us that our worship is meant to be sincere and led by the Spirit.

Worship is the natural response when you recognize God's faithfulness, mercy, and love. This doesn't have to be formal, organized, or planned. Worship is as simple as turning your eyes toward him, offering him your praise, and listening when he speaks. Giving him lordship in your life is an act of worship. Filling your heart with the Word is an act of worship. Directing your thoughts toward his goodness is an act of worship. Each day is filled with a multitude of opportunities to worship the Father in spirit and in truth.

Worship the Lord with your choices today.

Healer

Jesus was going about in all Galilee, teaching in their synagogues and proclaiming the gospel of the kingdom, and healing every disease and every sickness among the people.

MATTHEW 4:23 NASB

Jesus was not simply a great teacher or rabbi in the days of his ministry. He moved in power, reaching people with the tangible love of God through signs and wonders. He healed broken bodies, driving sickness from those who were ill. The gospel of his kingdom is still revealed through the power of God meeting us in miracles.

Refuse to stay small in your prayer life even when you don't receive the answers you want. Instead of letting disappointment weigh down your heart, may you press into the substantial presence of God. Jesus is still a healer even when it doesn't happen according to your timeline. He is the resurrected one, and his power is as potent today as it was when he walked this earth.

Pray for someone's healing today.

Listen

"Those who listen with open hearts will receive more revelation. But those who don't listen with open hearts will lose what little they think they have!"

MARK 4:25 TPT

Humility lends to our growth. When we recognize that we don't have it all together, we see humanity in each other without the need for comparison. Humility keeps our hearts soft, but pride leaves us with rocky and impenetrable ground. Through humility, the soil of our hearts is ready for the nourishment of God's wisdom.

Instead of seeking to be heard today, strive to listen. Be attentive and thoughtful while other people are speaking. Don't listen with the intent to respond but with the intent to understand. Show compassion by deliberately showing interest in what someone is saying. You display God's kindness when you listen well.

Practice being a good listener today.

Love in Action

This is the love of God, that we keep his commandments. And his commandments are not burdensome.

1 John 5:3 ESV

God asks us to follow his ways and honor his Word with our actions. We can't deny that he asks us to live a certain way. Scripture outlines his standards, and we would be remiss to say that he doesn't care how we live. 1 John reveals a truth that we must keep in mind. We are meant to follow his commands, and his commands are not burdensome. In other words, he asks us to be obedient, and he gives us everything we need to do it.

God has given you grace to follow every single one of his commands. He doesn't ask you to do anything that cannot be done. He is not unreasonable, and he is not a dictator. You have everything you need to live a life that honors him. There's no need to carry burdens that he hasn't asked you to. Lean on him, trust him, and don't take a single step without his grace.

What does obedience to God look like for you today?

Unashamed

Hope does not put us to shame, because God's love has been poured into our hearts through the Holy Spirit who has been given to us.

Romans 5:5 ESV

Hope will not put us to shame. In other words, we will not be disappointed by God's promises. He has already fulfilled his covenant by sending his Son to die for us. He has already proven himself to be faithful by redeeming us and setting us free. We can stand firmly upon everything he's done and look toward the future with confident hope.

Following the Lord is always the right choice. Nothing is wasted in his kingdom. If you devote your life to him, every single moment counts. He is worth everything you have, and you won't be left empty handed. Today, thank him for how he's poured his love into your heart and continue to trust him for what's to come.

Let hope rise without trying to temper it in yourself or others.

Satisfied

"God blesses those who hunger and thirst for justice, for they will be satisfied."

MATTHEW 5:6 NLT

Our desire for justice will be satisfied. For every cause that we feel passionate about, we can trust that God cares even more than we do. He mourns over the injustice in the world, and he promises to satisfy our desire for things to be made right. It's important that we trust him to fulfill his Word. We set ourselves up for failure and disappointment when we insist on curating justice for ourselves.

God is not ignoring injustice. He is fully aware of every single person who has been overlooked, oppressed, or unfairly burdened. You can trust that he will uplift them and care for them perfectly. He promises to make all things right, and you can lean on that promise when you feel discouraged by what's going on around you.

Follow God's leadership in your desire for justice.

Let Go of Worry

Give all your worries and cares to God, for he cares about you.

1 Peter 5:7 NLT

We don't have to carry our burdens alone. Holding onto our worries or ruminating on them won't do anything except keep us trapped in unfruitful patterns of thinking. Just because a worry pops up in our minds doesn't mean we have to carry the weight of it ourselves. We can develop the habit of passing our worries on to God as soon as they come up.

The most productive thing you can do with anxiety is give it to God. Cast your cares upon him, and trust that he knows what to do with them. He can carry your worries, and he can offer you wisdom and peace. He doesn't just take them from you and give you nothing in return. He cares for you, and he eagerly provides for you.

Give God your worries today. Rest in his love.

Settled by Grace

May the God of all grace, who called us to His eternal glory by Christ Jesus, after you have suffered a while, perfect, establish, strengthen, and settle you.

1 Peter 5:10 NKJV

Though we may suffer grief, pain, and loss, the Lord will never abandon us in our weakness. He is close at all times, and he holds us together. He is the God of all grace, and he knows exactly what we need. He has more than enough power to perfect, fill, establish, strengthen, and settle us. He does not leave us to waste away in our suffering.

May the God of all grace fill you with his lavish mercy today. Yesterday was not the end of your story and today is not a lost cause. Take time to dwell on your history with God. Do you see how he has delivered you time and time again? He is with you in the valleys, and he is present at each height. Wherever you are, he is already there. Take heart and find hope in his present nearness today.

Acknowledge where God's love has brought beauty out of your troubles.

Even Greater

If, while we were enemies, we were reconciled to God through the death of his Son, then how much more, having been reconciled, will we be saved by his life.

Romans 5:10 CSB

God reconciled himself to us while we were still his enemy. He didn't wait for us to get our lives together or clean up our acts. He wasn't disillusioned as to who we were or how we would respond. He risked everything fully knowing that some people would reject him. He saw our sin clearly, yet he still made a way for us to be near to him.

God didn't let your sin get in the way of calling you his own. Don't create your own barriers by allowing your flaws to dictate how you interact with God. If you have called upon his name, he has reconciled you to himself. He offers you freedom, peace, and the hope of resurrection.

Allow God to rescue you anew today.

Built Up

Encourage one another and build one another up, just as you are doing.

1 Thessalonians 5:11 ESV

There is incredible strength in the encouragement we give and receive from others. Our spirits are strengthened when we call out the goodness of God in each other. We should look for ways to build each other up in love whenever we have the opportunity. The kingdom of God is one of abundance, so let's give away reassurance and encouragement without holding back.

Do your friends know what you appreciate about them? Does your family know how much you love them? Do your fellow believers know that you are rooting for them? Each day is an opportunity to build others up in the love of God. Deliberately point out the strengths of others. Notice when people are upset and give them the gift of a listening ear. Reassure those who are weak, and use your words, time, and resources to bolster those who are hurting.

Call a friend and encourage them.

Confident Communion

We are confident that he hears us whenever we ask for anything that pleases him.

1 John 5:14 NLT

We have been brought near to the heart of God through fellowship with Christ. We are not at a distance, and we don't need to wonder whether or not he hears us. We are fully known by God, and we have his attention. We don't have to compete with others for an audience before him because his capacity is endless.

Take courage as you come to Jesus today. He sees you as you are, and he accepts you in his love. There is nothing you could offer him that he would be shocked by. There is nothing you could say to deter his mercy. Give him all that you are, and his love will reach the depths of your soul. Be bold in your prayers today, asking for more than you typically do. There's no need to filter yourself with God. He loves it when you come to him!

Pray without a filter today.

Beyond Description

The Lord's greatness is beyond description,
and he deserves all the praise that comes to him.
He is our King-God, and it's right
to be in holy awe of him.

Psalm 96:4 TPT

Gratitude is a form of worship. It is good and right to acknowledge God's work in our lives and declare his goodness for all to hear. He deserves all our praise, and he is worthy of everything we have to offer. As we appreciate who he is, our hearts are softened and we come into alignment with him.

Practice the habit of gratitude. Offer your heartfelt worship to God by telling him what you are thankful for. Thank him for his obvious gifts and thank him for the promises that have yet to be fulfilled. Thank him for his provision in the past and thank him for every small blessing you've experienced throughout your days.

Cultivate gratitude by making a list of things you are thankful for.

Fresh Start

If anyone is in Christ, he is a new creation. The old has passed away; behold, the new has come.

1 Corinthians 5:17 ESV

When we say yes to Jesus we are given a fresh start. We are no longer defined by our old habits, choices, or brokenness. No matter what our past holds, the best is yet to come. We can depend on Jesus to set our feet on solid ground, restore what is broken, and fill us with hope for the future.

Do you live as though you are a new creation? While it's good to learn and grow from past mistakes, it's not necessary to carry guilt and shame. The reality is that guilt prevents you from finding true restoration. Jesus offers you a different way. Allow him to lead you toward healing in every area of your life. He will give you peace, wisdom, and a path forward.

Leave your shame in the hands of Jesus today.

Fresh Air

Anyone who belongs to Christ has become a new person. The old life is gone; a new life has begun!

2 Corinthians 5:17 NLT

When we surrender to Jesus, we become new. We are set free and no longer need to live under the burden of sin. We can let go of old habits, tendencies, and ways of thinking. We can trust Jesus to lead us toward healing, wholeness, and reconciliation. He faithfully teaches us how to apply the Word to our lives and let truth set us free.

It can be difficult to let go of the past, but it is worth it. Don't hinder yourself by holding onto mistakes, regrets, and your old way of living. Let Jesus transform your heart with his love and restore whatever is broken. Turn to him with anticipation, knowing that from the moment you surrender to him he faithfully leads you toward eternal life.

Is there any area of your past you've been holding on to?

In Everything

In everything give thanks; for this is the will of God for you in Christ Jesus.

1 Thessalonians 5:18 NASB

Scripture calls us to give thanks in everything. We can thank God at all times no matter what our circumstances are. The more we look to him with gratitude in our hearts, the more we will establish the practice of thanksgiving. Eventually it will be a cemented habit that puts us in continual alignment with God's heart and purposes.

Building a habit takes time and intentionality. You don't need to start with the end goal in mind. Give yourself realistic goals with realistic timelines. Think of one reason per day to be thankful. Don't worry about whether it's big or small. Offer the Lord the first thing that comes to mind. As you continue to look for reasons to be thankful, you'll find yourself noticing them everywhere.

Practice saying thank you to God throughout your day.

Reunions of Mercy

All of this is a gift from God, who brought us back to himself through Christ. And God has given us this task of reconciling people to him.

2 Corinthians 5:18 NLT

The world is full of war, division, and disagreement. Everywhere we look we see people battling over one thing or another. This is not the way of Christ. He calls us to be ministers of reconciliation. By displaying his love and peace for all to see, we can show others who God is.

It's not always easy to be a peacemaker, but it is always worth it. It's not always comfortable to extend grace to others, but it is what you are called to do. It's not always convenient to spend your time building bridges, but it is valuable and meaningful work. Today, remember that if God has called you to do something, he has also given you everything you need to accomplish it.

Take steps to unify others rather than allowing divisions to drive people further apart.

Powerful Name

Give thanks for everything to God the Father in the name of our Lord Jesus Christ.

EPHESIANS 5:20 NLT

When we treat each day as the gift it is, we are able to more readily find the small blessings hidden in our lives. Cultivating a heart of gratitude allows us to hear birdsong, take in a sunset, and revel in laughter. God has given us so many wonderful gifts. His goodness is everywhere.

What simple joys bring you satisfaction? Is it conversation with a good friend who knows you without explanation? Is it the companionship of a loyal pet? Is it the way the evening light reflects off the water? Whatever it is that brings you joy, give thanks to God. Let the name of Jesus be on your lips throughout your day and thank him for the mercies that are present in your life.

Remember Jesus throughout your day.

Today Is the Day

God says, "At just the right time, I heard you. On the day of salvation, I helped you." Indeed, the "right time" is now. Today is the day of salvation.

2 Corinthians 6:2 nlt

God's timing is perfect. He is not slow, late, or early. He sees the entire trajectory of the universe, and he knows precisely when to show up. He is a perfect and wise judge. We can trust him to move in exactly the right way at exactly the right time.

There is no need to question the timing of God. His ability to orchestrate your life goes far beyond your own. You can trust him with every moment of every day, knowing that he is in control. He sees you, hears you, and will help you whenever he sees fit. Trust his wisdom, and take a deep breath, knowing that you are in capable hands.

Choose not to fret over timing today.

Spring Rains

"Let us acknowledge the LORD;
let us press on to acknowledge him.
As surely as the sun rises,
he will appear;
he will come to us like the winter rains,
like the spring rains that water the earth."

HOSEA 6:3 NIV

When we learn to acknowledge the Lord in everything, our hearts grow in the practice of gratitude. Let us not grow tired of looking for ways to recognize his work in our lives. He is more faithful than the sunrise. He is more reliable than the changing of the seasons. He is glorious, and he is always at work in us.

The Lord is with you, but you haven't yet experienced the fullness of his goodness. A day is coming when you will see him face to face. On that day, he will restore everything that has been lost. He will wipe away every tear, and he will heal every part of you that is broken. Until that day comes, look for the ways that he faithfully shows himself in the world around you.

Thank God for the multitude of gifts around you.

Satisfaction in Simplicity

True godliness with contentment is itself great wealth.

1 TIMOTHY 6:6 NLT

There is tremendous beauty and satisfaction in finding serenity in the present moment. Perfection and ease may not be possible in every season of the soul, but contentment is. With our hearts surrendered to the love of God, following his ways and his leading, we can experience the fullness of his presence. There is always a reason to celebrate his present goodness, for he is our abundant portion.

Look for simple joys throughout your day and give thanks for each one. There is light even in the harshest circumstances. The stars shine brightly even in the darkest night. There is living water to quench your thirst. There is nourishment for your soul in the Word of God. There is fresh air to breathe, sun to warm your skin, and there is hope in the rains of spring. Look for where mercy meets you, and you will find the fingerprints of God in your life.

How can you cultivate contentment in your life?

Faithful Father

"Your Father knows exactly what you need even before you ask him!"

Matthew 6:8 NLT

We don't ask God for things because he is unaware of our needs. He knows exactly how to provide for us. We ask him for help because it cultivates a meaningful and personal relationship with him. We run to him in prayer because it's a declaration of our dependence upon him. Our willingness to ask him for our needs shows that we understand his greatness and the frailty of our position.

God is attentive, kind, and always willing to help you. He knows you fully, and he longs for you to depend upon him. As you lean on him, he is able to guide you along the best path for your life. As you look to him for strength, he is able to give you perseverance for whatever you might face. As you humble yourself before him, he is able to lift you up in his perfect timing.

Run to God with boldness and tell him what you need.

God's Will

He has told you, o man, what is good,
and what does the LORD require of you.
But to do justice, and to love kindness,
and to walk humbly with your God.

MICAH 6:8 ESV

It's common among Christian circles to overcomplicate the will of God. We think we need to have every step of our lives figured out, and we assume that people with a clear vision are faithfully living out their calling. The truth is that God has clearly laid out his expectations in Scripture. He cares far more about the way we live than the titles we have.

Micah outlines God's requirements without mincing words. God wants you to do justice, love kindness, and walk humbly before him. The details of how that plays out will differ from person to person, but the heart of the matter is the same. Your life doesn't need to fit nicely inside a specific box. Instead, keep your heart soft before the Lord and he will not let your foot slip.

How can you live up to God's requirements today?

And Yet

Our hearts ache, but we always have joy. We are poor, but we give spiritual riches to others. We own nothing, and yet we have everything.

2 Corinthians 6:10 NLT

God can create fruit in our lives regardless of our circumstances. When sorrow is heavy, he can give us joy. When we don't have material items to share, we can generously share the gifts of the kingdom. When life is filled with trials, we can have hope for what's to come. In Christ, we are not limited to our current, earthly reality.

Ask God to give you eyes to see beyond your physical circumstances. As you learn to focus on the truth of the kingdom rather than the details of your days, you'll begin to experience the blessings of God's riches. Even when you think you have nothing, you have everything through him. Your life is filled with abundant gifts.

When you are distracted by what you lack, remember what you already have.

No Longer Bound

Sin is no longer your master, for you no longer live under the requirements of the law. Instead, you live under the freedom of God's grace.

ROMANS 6:14 NLT

We have all been called to live under the freedom of God's grace. We have been given freedom from sin. Sin used to control our choices, shape our identity, and keep us bound in shame. Romans 6 calls us down a different path. Now we are liberated and free to live in the fullness of God's love for us.

Sin is no longer your master. You have the freedom to choose how you will live. You don't have to make choices that harm you or your loved ones. Instead, God gives an abundance of grace. He has equipped you to live a life that honors him. His ways are best, and he mercifully empowers you to follow him.

Remember that God has equipped you in every way.

December

You have taken away my clothes of mourning
and clothed me with joy,
that I might sing praises to you
and not be silent.
O Lord my God,
I will give you thanks forever!

Psalm 30:11-12 NLT

Just Grace

Each time he said, "My grace is all you need. My power works best in weakness." So now I am glad to boast about my weaknesses, so that the power of Christ can work through me.

2 Corinthians 12:9 NLT

God's power works best in weakness. This is a key point of the gospel. In order to recognize what Jesus has done for us we must be aware of our great need for him. If we are blind to our weaknesses or overwhelmed by them, we won't turn to him in gratitude or expectation.

Ruminating on your weaknesses is just as counterproductive as being pridefully unaware of them. Neither situation results in surrender. Noticing your weaknesses isn't enough. If you want to see the power of God at work, you'll need to invite him to move in your life. Keep your heart soft and readily offer him your life.

Thank God for your weakness today, recognizing there is more room for his grace to work.

In Due Time

"God blesses you who are hungry now,
for you will be satisfied.
God blesses you who weep now,
for in due time you will laugh."

Luke 6:21 NLT

On hard days, when sadness washes over us and we cannot shake off discouragement, what is our response? Do we shame ourselves for feeling down? Do we feel as though we are missing the mark? Happiness is not equivalent to godliness. God can handle our weakness and the tangled mess of our emotions.

When you are weak, God will be your strength. Give him the honest reality of your struggles when they arise. Let him take the weight of your worries and disappointment. Nothing is too heavy for the Lord to carry. He does not want your false positivity; he wants you as you are. In all things, look to the Lord. He is near, and he will help you.

Don't give up hope. Look to the Lord today.

Highly Valued

"Look at all the birds—do you think they worry about their existence? They don't plant or reap or store up food, yet your heavenly Father provides them each with food. Aren't you much more valuable to your Father than they?"

Matthew 6:26 TPT

If we can learn anything from nature, may it be that worry is unnecessary. Though we are prone to worrying, we don't need to live under its weight. Our minds are transformed in the power of Christ, and we are empowered by his grace to capture our thoughts and put them up to the light of his love.

You are a child of the Most High God. You are even more valuable than the birds of the air, the flowers of the field, or the beasts of the forest. The Lord highly values you. The one who created the stars, the earth, and everything in the universe is the one who formed you. Look through the lens of his love today and see yourself as he sees you.

Give your worries to God today.

Great Joy

The angel said to them, "Do not be afraid. I bring you good news that will cause great joy for all the people. Today in the town of David a Savior has been born to you; he is the Messiah, the Lord."

Luke 2:10-11 NIV

The beginning of Christ's life could not have been more humble. He was born into a normal and struggling family. He did not enjoy lavish circumstances, and he was not welcomed with extravagance or even comfort. He was born in a room filled with animals, and he was rejected from the very beginning.

In this humble introduction to life, Jesus was as dependent on his parents as any vulnerable newborn. As he grew and matured, he also grew in wisdom. He was a normal boy with a normal upbringing, yet he was the Savior of the world. What great news! This boy-turned-man would be the hope of every longing soul. Praise the Lord!

Read about Jesus' youth through the lens of his humanity.

Show Them

"You must be compassionate,
just as your Father is compassionate."

Luke 6:36 NLT

Jesus' instruction that we show mercy and compassion for others is a reminder that God the Father is full of love. He is kind to all, and he overflows with abundant mercy toward all that he has made. How will those who do not know the love of God be introduced to it unless we live it out?

You have been called to live a life of mercy and compassion. This is what it looks like to live the gospel of Christ. You cannot claim to follow him if you don't embrace a life of love and sacrifice. Allow your heart to be transformed by God and you will naturally overflow with mercy and grace toward others. May you continue to receive the depths of his love and to live it out with generosity.

Let compassion be the aim of your interactions with others today.

No Matter What

"All that the Father gives me will come to me, and whoever comes to me I will never cast out."

John 6:37 ESV

There is deep comfort in knowing that Jesus never turns anyone away. No matter what our lives look like or what mistakes we've made in the past, he is always available. His arms are always open, and he is eager to receive us. His promise of loyalty stirs up profound gratitude within our hearts.

There is nothing you can do to make God love you less. He will never ignore, overlook, or reject you. He promises that every single time you turn to him, he will respond with love, mercy, and grace. Let his faithful love fill you with a sense of security. Thank him for his steady and reliable love.

Thank the Lord for his faithful presence in your life.

No More Judging

"Do not judge, and you will not be judged.
Do not condemn, and you will not be condemned.
Forgive, and you will be forgiven."

Luke 6:37 CSB

Criticism is not a fruit of the Spirit, and neither is judgment of others. If we spend our energy picking others apart, we miss seeing how they display God's glory. None of us is perfect, though we are trying our best in life. With grace as our motto, may we offer each other the benefit of the doubt. May we choose to forgive, even when others refuse to change. May we overlook a multitude of flaws, know that we ourselves are far from perfect.

When you live with patience, kindness, and peace, you allow room for the humanity of others. May you set aside unrealistic and perfectionistic standards and offer the humble love of Jesus instead. Consider how you want to be treated and treat others in that way. Give others the opportunity to repair, restore, and transform just as God gives you that same opportunity on a daily basis.

When you begin to criticize someone in your heart today, invite grace to change your perspective.

Filled to Overflow

I am filled with comfort. In all our affliction, I am overflowing with joy.

2 Corinthians 7:4 ESV

In the midst of deep grief, the Lord is still full of abundant love. May we be filled with the comfort of his presence. May we know the deep, abiding joy of his tender care. No matter the trial, no matter how deeply entrenched we are in pain, God is still the same powerful and merciful God that he has always been. The persistent peace of his presence is a deep well that will never run dry.

Today, no matter where this finds you, turn to the Lord. He is abundant in kindness, and his peace surpasses your understanding of it. He is with you in all your afflictions. He is near when you are disappointed and alone. Rest in his presence and rejoice in the steadiness of his character.

Offer encouragement to someone who is struggling today.

Generations of Mercy

"Know therefore that the LORD your God is God; he is the faithful God, keeping his covenant of love to a thousand generations of those who love him and keep his commandments."

DEUTERONOMY 7:9 NIV

We serve a faithful God. Faithfulness isn't just a singular aspect of his character. He is the embodiment of faithfulness. He never wavers, forgets, or breaks his promises. He makes covenants, and they last for eternity. He gives us his Word, and we can rest securely in it because it will never be broken.

When life feels uncertain, cling to the faithfulness of God. When you're unsure which way to go, you can depend on him. Let his steadfast faithfulness fill your heart with thanksgiving and admiration. Recognize his eternal loyalty and let it stir you to live a life of obedience and worship.

Acknowledge how God's faithfulness has played out through history and in your own life.

Christ's Compassion

When the Lord saw her, his heart overflowed with compassion. "Don't cry!" he said.

LUKE 7:13 NLT

When Jesus spoke to the widow in Luke he didn't tell her to stop crying because he was bothered by her tears or because she didn't have a good reason to cry. He told her to stop crying, and he stepped in and brought her dead son back to life. When Jesus asks us to do something, he always equips us and walks alongside us.

God sees your tears. He doesn't shame you for your feelings, and he doesn't demand that you pull yourself together. He offers you compassion, and he reminds you of the truth. He intervenes on your behalf, and he displays his faithfulness. If he has asked you to something, he will move alongside you.

Thank God for his compassionate and faithful love.

Continue

Each one of you should continue to live the way God has given you to live—the way you were when God called you.

1 Corinthians 7:17 NCV

It's easy to get caught up in the belief that joy and purpose are elusive. We think we'll find them if we just change that specific thing we don't like about our life. If we get a different job, move into a better house, or get through our current stage of life, maybe we'll be satisfied. This way of thinking will only lead to dissatisfaction and frustration.

God has called you to live according to his purposes. His requirements can be satisfied anywhere, anytime, and in any phase of life. He doesn't ask you to achieve certain goals, mold your life in a particular way, or make sure you have a specific level of success. He asks for your surrendered and devoted heart. His purposes in your life have very little to do with your physical circumstances. There is nothing holding you back from living exactly the way God has called you to live.

Continue to offer God thanks through your submitted life.

Habit of Praise

I will thank the Lord because he is just;
I will sing praise to the name of the Lord Most High.

Psalm 7:17 TPT

Gratitude is more than a feeling; it's something we are called to actively express to the Lord. We are meant to declare our thanks to him. This takes intentionality and sometimes discipline. We won't always feel grateful. Sometimes it's downright difficult to think of something we are thankful for. In those times the act of thanksgiving is what transforms our perspective.

Gratitude is a habit you can develop. The more you do it, the more it will feel like second nature. As you turn toward God in thanksgiving, you'll begin to notice his goodness everywhere. You'll see it in areas you previously overlooked, and your heart will steadily overflow with praise.

Look for reasons to praise God in an area you've typically overlooked.

Fully Free

There is therefore now no condemnation for those who are in Christ Jesus.

ROMANS 8:1 ESV

There is no need for our souls to be weighed down by guilt and shame. Jesus paid our debts, and he offers us eternal freedom. He has forgiven our sins, and he continuously renews us whenever we run to him. There is no limit to the number of times we can repent and fully expect him to wipe our slate clean. There is not a single ounce of condemnation for us when we let Jesus have lordship in our lives.

Don't forget the miraculous simplicity of the gospel. Through Christ, you are redeemed. He cleansed you of all sin, and he continues to carry your burdens. When guilt threatens to overtake you, cast it into his capable hands. When shame begins to creep into your heart, refuse to give in and stand firmly upon the strong foundation of Christ's love. The freedom he has purchased for you cannot be taken from you.

Remember that God does not hold anything against you today.

Nothing Impossible

This is what the LORD of Heaven's Armies says: "All this may seem impossible to you now, a small remnant of God's people. But is it impossible for me?" says the LORD of Heaven's Armies.

ZECHARIAH 8:6 NLT

With the Lord, all things are possible. He is not discouraged by our complicated situations. Though we may not know what to do, God does. His wisdom is perfect, and his judgment is sound. His perception is clear, and his understanding goes far beyond our own. He is mighty and strong, and he is willing to intervene on our behalf.

Try reframing your thoughts today when you are presented with an overwhelming situation. Instead of letting helplessness drive you to dread, get excited for what God will do. He will not let anything in your life go to waste. He can do far more than you can even imagine him doing! Pray and ask him for help, trusting him to follow through.

Trust God with the impossible situations in your life.

Gracious Giving

You are rich in everything—in faith, in speaking, in knowledge, in truly wanting to help, and in the love you learned from us. In the same way, be strong also in the grace of giving.

2 Corinthians 8:7 NCV

When Paul wrote to the Corinthian church he praised them for the many areas they excelled in. Their faith was strong, they loved each other well, and they spoke the truth. He goes on to encourage them to pursue the same level of excellence in the area of giving. This tells us that generosity is just as important as having a strong faith or loving others well.

Generosity can accomplish so many things in your life. As you keep your hands open, you acknowledge that God is the source of your provision. As you give what you have, you create an opportunity to further trust him for your needs. As you share without expectation, you cultivate kindness in your relationships. God can use generosity to keep your heart soft and your eyes on him.

Strive to give freely as God has given freely to you.

Extravagant Love

Many waters cannot quench love;
rivers cannot sweep it away.
If one were to give all the wealth
of one's house for love,
it would be utterly scorned.

SONG OF SOLOMON 8:7 NIV

God's love is so deep and powerful that nothing can overcome it. His love for us is unquenchable. There is no hardship, distance, or amount of time that can diminish the power of God's great love. It is fierce, faithful, and enduring. Through Christ we have the incredible privilege of experiencing God's love without limitations.

You are loved with a love that never gives up, runs dry, or lets go. You are loved so passionately and faithfully by your Creator. He looks at you with mercy and grace, and he longs for you to understand his love for you. Everything he does in your life is based on a firm foundation of love. Each day is a new opportunity for you to marvel at the incredible love of God.

Let God's love fill you with wonder and awe today.

Light of Life

"I am the Light of the world; he who follows Me will not walk in the darkness, but will have the Light of life."

John 8:12 NASB

Darkness can be overwhelming. It amplifies confusion, anxiety, and fear of the unknown. Burdens feel even heavier in the dark, and it can feel impossible to maintain hope that the sun will ever rise. The good news for believers is that Jesus steps into our darkness and declares that he is our true source of life.

Walk in the brilliant light of Christ's presence today. Remember that he illuminates the darkest parts of your heart and life. He declares that through him you have redemption, purpose, and hope. He does not leave you alone to stumble toward the light. He himself causes his love to shine brightly and drive away the darkness.

Invite Jesus to shine his light on every part of your life.

It Will Be Clear

"Nothing is hidden that will not be made manifest, nor is anything secret that will not be known and come to light."

Luke 8:17 ESV

Nothing done in secret will remain a secret forever. Dark deeds committed with deceit and pride will not go unnoticed. God will hold us accountable, and he will not let the shadows conceal what he sees clearly. Do not despair in your commitment to integrity. Do not give up doing the right thing in love, though others may not take notice. God sees, he knows, and he will not let it go to waste.

When you are presented with the opportunity to take the easy way out, consider that God still sees. Don't be tricked into thinking that little lies don't mean anything. Live your life with honesty and continue to follow the leadership of the Lord. Integrity is worth the sacrifice of momentary ease. Live for the audience of the Lord and commit your life to him alone.

Choose to do the right thing even if no one is watching.

Help for Today

The Spirit also helps our weakness; for we do not know what to pray for as we should, but the Spirit Himself intercedes for us with groanings too deep for words.

ROMANS 8:26 NASB

The Spirit is our help in every moment. The fellowship we have with the Lord is uninterrupted and unhindered. Let us not rely on our own waning strength when we have access to the great grace of God through his Spirit. Even when we do not know how to pray, the Spirit intercedes for us. There is nothing that we are alone in.

You don't need to strive alone in any area of your life. Lean into the overwhelming goodness of your constant companion and help today. Depend on him in your joys and in your disappointments. God is the source of everything you need. Run to him with an open heart, open minds, and a yielded life. That is where you will find your overcoming strength.

Lean into the Spirit in prayer today.

Uncontainable

"Will God indeed dwell on the earth? Behold, heaven and the highest heaven cannot contain You, how much less this house which I have built!"

1 Kings 8:27 NASB

When we try to fit God into our understanding, we diminish his greatness and power. There is nothing that he cannot do. The earth cannot contain him, nor can the vast expanse of space. He is grander than our capacity to grasp. He is more wonderful than we can dream. May we allow his love to broaden our perspective and fill us with awe.

God is both greater than you can know and nearer than you realize. He is not bound by flesh and bones. He is the Spirit, and he moves freely. He is not limited by anything. Devote your life to worshipping him and seeking his glory. He alone is worthy of everything you have.

Acknowledge that God is greater than your circumstances.

Woven into Purpose

We know that all things work together for the good of those who love God, who are called according to his purpose.

ROMANS 8:28 CSB

Life doesn't always meet our expectations. We experience loss, disappointments, and unexpected hurdles. There is solace in the fact that even our let downs can be woven into a story that ultimately glorifies God. Every part of our lives, the good and the bad, can be incorporated into God's perfect plan. His purposes are greater than the details of our days.

The reality of God's sovereignty doesn't erase the sting of disappointment, but it can help cultivate gratitude. When you realize that God is working everything together for your good, your heart begins to soften. You can recognize his overarching plan and lift your eyes beyond your current circumstances.

Trust that God will use every detail of your life for your good and for his glory.

Better Way

What should we say then? Since God is on our side, who can be against us?

ROMANS 8:31 NCV

When life is difficult or our relationships cause strife, it's easy to let anger or bitterness take root in our hearts. Romans 8 reminds us that there is a better way. Instead, we can focus on the fact that God is for us. Our Creator is on our side, and he strengthens us whenever we need it. He offers us wisdom to navigate the most difficult situations, and he gives us grace to love others beyond our abilities.

People may hurt you and life might feel unfair, but at the end of the day the truth remains. God is with you at all times. He is faithful, and he is on your side. He will not abandon you, and he will not leave you to struggle alone. Today, choose to respond to hurt or disappointment with gratitude for God's constant companionship and help.

Rest in the confidence of God's faithfulness today.

Good Father

Since he did not spare even his own Son but gave him up for us all, won't he also give us everything else?

Romans 8:32 NLT

God didn't hold back his Son, so why would he hold back anything else we need? He willingly gave up his most precious possession so that we could experience the perfection of his presence. God's sacrificial love is the greatest gift we will ever receive. We can trust him to take care of us because he has proven himself faithful through Christ.

The more you reflect on what God has done for you, the less room you have for frustration or resentment. As you focus on God's generosity and mercy, your heart will remain soft and thankful. Instead of dwelling on your disappointments, your perspective will shift. You'll find it easier to forgive, release offense, and live by grace.

Ask what the Lord has for you today and receive it with an open heart.

Liberated

"If the Son sets you free, you are truly free."

John 8:36 NLT

Freedom in Christ is more than a nice spiritual idea. It's the reality of our lives if we've surrendered to him. We have been set free from the weight of sin and death. We have unlimited access to the grace and forgiveness of our Father. Through Christ, we are not lacking anything.

Everything changes when you allow the freedom Christ offers you to permeate your entire life. You can confidently walk along the path God has set before you because he has given you everything you need. you don't need to worry about taking a wrong turn or making mistakes because his love covers a multitude of sins. You can pursue his purposes with boldness because he has given you grace to do it. You are free to live without shame, guilt, and worry.

Make your choices today as one who is truly free.

Wonderful Leader

"A child has been born to us; God has given a son to us. He will be responsible for leading the people. His name will be Wonderful Counselor, Powerful God, Father Who Lives Forever, Prince of Peace."

Isaiah 9:6 NCV

Jesus is the best leader. He is full of wisdom, peace, and love. He is the wisest counselor we will ever know. He is the most powerful force in the universe. He is the bodily expression of the eternal Father. He is the Prince of peace. There is no shortage of mercy in his heart. Nothing is impossible for him.

Do you trust God to guide you in his goodness? Have you known his faithfulness toward you? He is loyal to his Word, and he is still speaking today. May you know the confidence of his presence through his Spirit within you. He gives revelation to expand your understanding of his kingdom. He speaks in simple and profound truth. Spend time in his Word and ask him to reveal greater depths of understanding.

Submit to Jesus' leadership today, trusting his goodness to guide you.

Declare His Goodness

"Go back to your family, and tell them everything God has done for you." So he went all through the town proclaiming the great things Jesus had done for him.

Luke 8:39 NLT

When we declare what God has done for us, we not only remind ourselves of his goodness, but we also invite others into it. Our testimony becomes the invitation for others to experience the same. God's work in our lives is not isolated. He longs for everyone to recognize the power of his love in their own stories.

Take the words of Jesus seriously, knowing that he has intention behind everything he says. We are meant to share our lives with those around us. That includes sharing the good news of Jesus. When God's mercy meets you in tangible ways, don't keep it to yourself. You were made to share your victories and to encourage one another in faith. How can you declare God's goodness today?

Share what God has done for you with others.

Peace and Gratitude

Let the peace of Christ rule in your hearts, since as members of one body you were called to peace. And be thankful.

Colossians 3:15 NIV

Peace and gratitude work together. When we allow God's peace to rule our hearts, we will be unshakeable. As we remain grounded in his presence and assured of his provision, we will naturally overflow with thanksgiving. As we keep our eyes on the Lord, we will remain secure and confident in his presence.

Peace is found when you recognize the reality of God's kingdom despite your physical circumstances. This means trusting in God's goodness no matter what is going on in your life. It means leaning on his faithfulness despite how you feel. Today, choose to rest in God's peace.

How can you deliberately choose peace today?

Cheerful Giving

Let giving flow from your heart, not from a sense of religious duty. Let it spring up freely from the joy of giving—all because God loves hilarious generosity!

2 Corinthians 9:7 TPT

God is not looking for our acts of obligation. We are not enslaved! We are children of the Most High, and we have freedom to choose how we will live and how we will give. God is a good Father who cares about the state of our hearts. He wants us to experience the joy of generosity more than he wants us to check an item off a list of expected actions.

When it comes to giving, God has offered you freedom to choose how you will do it. He loves a cheerful giver. Consider how you can lovingly reach out with tangible acts of kindness today. Decide what you can give and do it joyfully. Ask the Lord for his input, and you may be surprised at his suggestions.

Decide in your heart to intentionally give today and follow through on it.

His Provision

God is the one who provides seed for the farmer and then bread to eat. In the same way, he will provide and increase your resources and then produce a great harvest of generosity in you.

2 Corinthians 9:10 tpt

Have you considered lately that God has provided you with everything you have? He gives seed for the person who plants. He makes sure the hungry have something to eat. As we work with what we have, God blesses it. Everything that we do with diligence will reap a reward. Nothing goes to waste in his kingdom.

Acknowledge God's provision today. He is the author and perfecter of your faith. He is the one who has given you various skills and abilities. Don't put yourself on a pedestal when God is the one who has graciously given you everything you need. Thank him for everything he's done and humbly put your life into his hands.

Thank God for his help and work diligently at whatever he has given you.

Restoration Is Coming

"Return to the stronghold, you prisoners of hope. Even today I declare that I will restore double to you."

Zechariah 9:12 NKJV

God is our restorer. He gently takes what is broken and repairs it expertly. He is capable of holding each of our lives in his hands, and he is more than willing to bring restoration. Not only does he fix and mend, but he goes above and beyond what is needed. He blesses us far beyond what we can imagine.

Where hope has waned, look to the Lord. With God, all things are possible. His solutions are better than any you could come up with on your own. Rest in the confidence of his faithfulness as he turns the rubble of your disappointment into fields of glory. Surely, the best is yet to come.

Continue trusting God for breakthrough where you need it.

Have Courage

Be on your guard; stand firm in the faith;
be courageous; be strong.

1 Corinthians 16:13 NIV

We can all be uplifted by Paul's words in 1 Corinthians. At some point, we all need to be encouraged to simply keep going. We all become weary and are prone to doubt that we have what it takes. Paul reminds us that we are fully equipped to finish our race. Our Father has provided everything we need, and we are strong because of him.

Keep going! Don't quit! Even when you are tired of putting one foot in front of the other, God is able to strengthen you. In God's kingdom, standing firm actually means leaning on the steady foundation of his love rather than propping yourself up. Look to him for direction, and trust that he has your back.

Have courage! The Lord is with you!